THE
ANGLO-ISRAEL
THESIS

COMPELLING EVIDENCE THAT CAUCASIAN EUROPEANS DESCENDED FROM THE ANCIENT ISRAELITES

REED BENSON

The Anglo-Israel Thesis
Copyright © 2013
by Watchman Outreach Ministries

Printed in the United States of America

Published By:
Watchman Outreach Ministries
3161 South 2275 Road
Schell City, MO 64783

ISBN # 978-1481908955

For Michael.
May you be the first of many.

The Anglo-Israel Thesis
Compelling Evidence that Caucasian Europeans Descended from the Ancient Israelites

Preface

"Thou sleep'st, awake and see thyself."
—Shakespeare, *Julius Caesar*

Sharon Turner's seminal work, *The History of the Anglo-Saxons*, addressed in part the question of the identity of the White race of northwest Europe. Published in 1805 and meticulously researched from Roman and Greek primary sources, it is considered definite. He began his story of the Anglo-Saxon race when they entered the continent of Europe from the Caucasus Mountain range circa 600 B.C, hence the reason the White race is called "Caucasian." Turner states these energetic tribal nations were variously called Scythians, Goths, Gatae, Massagatae, and Sacae. He tracked them westward from the Caucasus into central and northwest Europe, where they became the dominant race by 200 B.C. But from where did they come before the Caucasus Mountain region?

A careful analysis of the Bible, the *Apocrypha*, Josephus' *Jewish Antiquities*, and a number of other ancient sources reveals that the Goths, Sacae, etc. who emerged from the north side of the Caucasus Mountains are none other than the so called "lost ten tribes of Israel" who disappeared into that mountain region from the south side in the seventh century before Christ. The cause of their sudden migration northward was the dissolution of the Assyrian Empire from which they were most eager to escape after being taken into captivity by the same. A century earlier the terrifying Assyrian military machine had destroyed the northern kingdom of Israel after three long campaigns. Over a period of some thirty years, vast numbers of Israelites had been forcibly relocated in the northern region of the Assyrian Empire immediately adjacent to the Caucasus. But when the Babylonians successfully overthrew the oppressive Assyrians, the captive Israelites seized their chance for freedom and bolted en masse northward over the mountains.

Thus the thesis is stated: Anglo-Saxon and kindred peoples of central and northwest Europe are direct genetic descendants of ancient Israel. Not only is this supported by historical documentation, but powerful evidence exists from Old Testament prophecy, New Testament epistles, archaeology, and linguistic analysis. There are those who resist the connective proof because they fear the implications. But should truth not be the highest calling? Will you study the evidence with an open mind? You who read this now, if you are of a Caucasian European background, a magnificent bequest awaits you.

What follows is not intended to be an exhaustive work, but rather a lucid, easy-to-read compilation of the essential elements of the Anglo-Israel thesis for those who have busy lives. If you are interested in greater depth, you can consult some of the books cited in the bibliography or contact *Watchman Outreach Ministries.*

Reed Benson
January 2013

1

Historical Evidence: The Tragic Tale of a Broken and Battered Nation

"Every living thing wants to survive."
–Spock, *Star Trek*, "The Ultimate Computer."

D o we believe something simply because we wish it to be true? Unfortunately, many people do just that. Some believe that the lost ten tribes of Israel are found among Negro tribes in Africa. Others sincerely argue that the Meso-Americans are the lost tribes. Still others suggest that they are in Japan. And, of course, many purport that they were simply absorbed into neighboring groups of people and were consequently permanently eradicated. In all truth, each of these positions is verifiably wrong.

So where are the lost ten tribes of Israel? What happened to these people? Using the Bible and careful, honest research, the direct descendants of the lost ten tribes can be identified. They are none other than the Anglo-Saxon people found primarily in northwest Europe. However, there were actually portions of *all twelve* tribes that were taken away from their original Israelite homeland. The tale of their forced deportation and slow migration to Europe is a bit tedious for those who do not care for details.

Yet, conclusions are only as good as the facts, and a detailed chain of historic data is necessary to yield a reliable result.

It is my hope that I can present enough of the details of the known story to persuade the reader that the bulk of the Lost Tribes are embodied in the Caucasian race of northwest Europe. The evidence is taken from four types of sources: first, the biblical record, which I consider inspired by God and thus without error. Second, primary sources, which are writers who were contemporary, or nearly so, to the events they were describing. The third source is historians of such long-standing reputation and universally acclaimed caliber that their studied opinion is considered expert. Fourth, we shall consider archaeological evidence and the local traditions associated with it, which sometimes provides unique insight.

Middle East Politics in the Eighth Century before Christ

Israel and Judah, the two nations of Israelites, had been politically separate for about two centuries. The northern kingdom, usually referred to as Israel, was larger in territory, population, and economic resources. Nine of the twelve tribes were spread across a fertile swath of land. (Simeon was somewhat scattered from its original geographical holdings.) Its ruling dynasties were unstable, however, and it had fallen into gross idolatry. It was ripe for God's judgment. The southern kingdom, Judah, was comprised of one large tribe, Judah; a small one, Benjamin; and remnants of Simeon, which had nearly dissolved. Poorer in natural resources, the southern kingdom had a smaller population of mostly pastoralists. However, it did boast the prosperous and historic city of Jerusalem and its ruling dynasty was unbroken since David. It was a conservative, traditional nation. Elements of the tribe of Levi were found in both the northern and southern kingdoms.

The two great powers of that period were the Assyrians to the northeast and the Egyptians to the southwest. Both Israel and Judah were forced to play a risky game of diplomacy to play these two great powers off one another as well as form temporary shifting alliances with their small neighbors in the hope

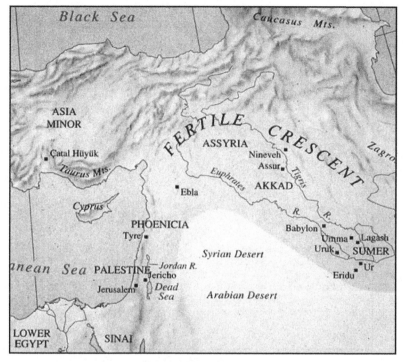

The Ancient Middle East, Eighth Century B.C.

of political advantage. As the century progressed, the power of Assyria grew, and the goal became one of finding allies to hold the mighty Assyrians back.

It is hard to imagine a more terrifying enemy than the ancient Assyrian war machine. They were the first in the history of warfare to make full use of what is now called combined arms which is the simultaneous use on the battlefield of infantry, archers, cavalry, and chariots. Assyria was unequalled in siege technology, using sappers to undermine city walls and a variety of devices to batter walls down. Efficiency and organization were their hallmark, being the first ancient military force to deploy specialized units for building bridges and hospital units to aid wounded comrades. Yet their military professionalism was not what captured the imagination of their adversaries. It was their policy of terror.

The Northern Kingdom of Israel
and the Southern Kingdom of Judah,
Eighth Century B.C.

Enemies that submittted immediately without resistance suffered only the indignity of defeat and mass deportation of all inhabitants. However, those that refused submission were held in special contempt when finally defeated. Executions of thousands was the routine, usually by one of their two favored methods: impalement or flaying. Impaling the victims was simple. Masses of large stakes were planted in the ground with the upper end sharpened. The offending prisoners were stripped of all clothing, elevated, and rammed down upon the sharp pole, ideally by shoving the stake through the anus into their vitals. If that were impractical, then simply poking the stake through the abdomen would suffice. Thus skewered like a hot dogs on sticks, the victims were left to slowly perish in shame and remorseless agony.

More creative was flaying. The victims were stripped of clothing, staked out on the ground in spread-eagle fashion, and then their skin was carefully peeled from their flesh. This tedious and horrifying process took more time and some specialized tools, but the Assyrians found its effects uniquely gratifying. By taking these human hides and stitching them into articles like umbrellas, they could be sported in front of other cities they were about to attack as an incentive to encourage immediate capitulation.

These were the Assyrians. This was the enemy that was pounding at the doors of the two Israelite nations.

The Assyrian Invasions: Phase One

The first important phase of Assyrian conquest over the Israelite nations was in 741 B.C. During the reign of Israel's King Pekah, Tiglath-pileser invaded the northern kingdom and captured all of the land east of the Jordan River and the fertile region around the Sea of Galilee. The two and one-half tribes east of the Jordan River, Reuben, Gad, and half of Manasseh, were taken into captivity, as well as portions of the tribes of Naphtali, Asher, and Zebulon that lived in the Galilee hill country. Dan,

An Assyrian archer, a member of the most advanced military machine in the world.

in the far north, was also almost certainly taken as it was quite vulnerable to attack from that direction. The biblical description of this invasion is found in 2 Kings 15:29: *"In the days of Pekah king of Israel came Tiglath-pileser king of Assyria, and took Ijon, and Abel-beth-maachah, and Janoah, and Kedesh, and Hazor, and Gilead, and Galilee, all the land of Naphtali, and carried them captive to Assyria."*

The surviving portion of the northern kingdom was Ephraim, Issachar, the western half of Manasseh, and the southern half of

Dan, as well as overlooked pockets of other northern tribes. The invasion might have been complete, but Pekah was assassinated by Hoshea, who took the throne and managed to secure a humiliating peace with the Assyrians.

The Bible specifically states where the tribes east of the Jordan River were taken: *"And the God of Israel stirred up the spirit of Pul king of Assyria, and the spirit of Tiglath-pileser king of Assyria, and he carried them away, even the Reubenites, and the Gadites, and the half tribe of Manasseh, and brought them unto Halah, and Habor, and Hara, and to the river Gozan, unto this day"* (1 Chonicles 5:26).

Assyrian terror:
flaying a captive alive.

The Assyrian Invasions: Phase Two

The next important advance of Assyrian military might into Israelite areas was completed in 721 B.C. Emperor Shalmaneser sent his forces, led by his commander and co-regent Sargon, to finish the conquest of the northern Israelite nation. After a horrific three-year siege of the capital city of Samaria, all resistance was crushed. An unknown number perished in the siege from famine and disease. All outlying areas that had been missed in the first invasion fell under the terrifying yoke of Assyrian dominion. Many people from these pockets were swept up and deported. Tobit, for example, a man from Naphtali who survived the first invasion, was taken in this one: *"This book tells the story of Tobit . . . of the tribe of Naphtali, who in the days of Shalmaneser of the Assyrians was taken into captivity from Thisbe, which is to the south of Kedesh Naphtali, in upper Galilee . . ." (Tobit 1:1-2, Apocrypha).*

Assyrian terror:
impaling captives alive.

The fall of Samaria was the final act in this successful campaign and is described in 2 Kings 18:10-11: ***"And at the end of three years they took it: even in the sixth year of Hezekiah, that is the ninth year of Hoshea king of Israel, Samaria was taken. And the king of Assyria did carry away Israel unto Assyria, and put them in Halah and in Habor by the river Gozan, and in the cities of the Medes."*** Sargon also recorded his activities: *"In the beginning of my reign the city of Samaria I besieged, I captured . . . 27,290 of its inhabitants I carried away"* (*The Ancient Records of Assyria and Babylon*, D.D. Luckenbill). These miserable survivors, according to the biblical record, joined their countrymen who had been taken away two decades earlier to Halah, Habor, by the River Gozan, and in the cities of Medes.

The Assyrian Invasions: Phase Three

The northern kingdom of the Israelites was no more. To fill the void, the Assyrians had imported *". . . Thamudites, the Ibadidites, the Marsiminiites, and the Khapaijans"* (ibid.).

These foreign and pagan peoples *"were transported to the midst of the land of Beth-Omri"* (ibid.) Beth-Omri means House of Omri, after one of the more prominent among the kings of the northern kingdom of Israel. The Bible records the importation of foreigners to replace the deported Israelites: *"And the king of Assyria brought men from Babylon, and from Cuthah, and from Ava, and from Hamath, and from Sepharvaim, and placed them in the cities of Samaria instead of the children of Israel" (2 Kings 17:24).* The mix of these various peoples in the region became the Samaritans of the New Testament.

While the southern kingdom of Judah still remained essentially intact, the Assyrian thirst for conquest had not been slaked. In 701 B.C. Sennacherib led a successful campaign along the coast of the Mediterranean Sea, capturing the Phoenecian city of Tyre and the Philistine cities of Ashkelon and Ekron. He then invaded Judah and captured, according to his records, forty-six walled cities of the southern kingdom. He had hoped to cap off this campaign with the capture of Jerusalem, but righteous Hezekiah appealed to Jehovah, and God heard his pleas. A death angel was sent to destroy the besieging Assyrian army around Jerusalem, massacring 185,000 (2 Kings 19:35-36; 2 Chronicles 32:1-23). The kingdom of Judah had been preserved, but not without a fearful cost. Sennacherib tried to cast as positive a light as possible on this campaign, stating that he had shut up Hezekiah and his army *"like a bird in a cage,"* and specifically stating that he carried away as captives 200,150 inhabitants of the forty-six Judean cities he captured (ibid).

Yet another subsequent invasion by Sennacherib's son Esar-Haddon in 676 B.C. forced Hezekiah's son Manasseh to yield completely to the Assyrians. However, Jerusalem was not destroyed, and although Judah became a subservient vassal state to the Assyrians, the nation, its institutions, and its people survived.

But what of the 200,150 Judean captives taken by Sennacherib? They were resettled in the northern reaches of the Assyrian empire alongside their brethren from the northern kingdom of Israel. There, in Halah, Habor, by the River Gozan, and in the land of the Medes, all twelve tribes of the children of Israel were resettled by the Assyrians. This was intended to be their permanent residence; separated from their ancient homeland and having had their former institutions and customs completely disrupted, the Assyrians believed they would remain quiescent.

Where Are Halah, Habor, Gozan, and the Land of the Medes?

This is not difficult to ascertain and information is available as close as the nearest Bible Dictionary. It was a region of the Assyrian Empire to the northwest of their capital city Ninevah. Gozan was a region called *Guzanu* by the Assyrians and *Gauzanitis* by the Roman historian Ptolemy. On the banks of this river, the German archaeologist Baron von Oppenheim discovered the ruins of the city of Halah, known today as Tell Halaf. The river today is not called Gozan, but is known as Khabur, after the ancient city of Habor. Today these locations are found in what is now the border area of southeast Turkey and northern Syria. Historians often refer to this area south of the Caucasus Mountains as Greater Armenia. The

Judean historian
Titus Flavius Josephus
(A.D. 37-100)

Khabur River is a tributary of the Euphrates; the irrigated area was capable of supporting a large population in ancient times. The entire northern portion of the Assyrian Empire, of which Halah, Habor, and Gozan were a part, was the land of the Medes. The Medes had been subjugated by the Assyrians and were eager to rebel against their cruel overlords. Later, in sixth century B.C., along with their cousins the Persians, the Medes established the Medo-Persian Empire. But by then a unqiue opportunity for the captive Israelites had already appeared, and most of them were gone. The Israelites had reasserted their independence and had relocated to a new region. The next phase of their national life was underway.

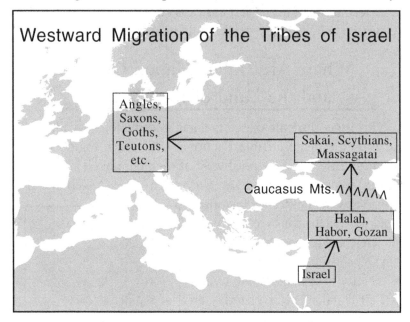

Westward Migration of the Tribes of Israel

Escape and Survival in a New and Distant Land

Where they went next is not as difficult to discern as some suggest. Ancient writers give us clear pieces of information. In 2 Esdras 13:40-45 we find this: *"These are the nine tribes that were taken away from their own land into exile in the days of Hoshea, whom Shalmaneser king of the Assyrians, made captives; he took them across the river, and they were taken into another land. But they formed this plan for themselves, that they would leave the multitude of the nations and go to a more distant region, where no human beings had ever lived, so that they might keep their statutes that they had not kept in their own land. And they went by the narrow passages of the Euphrates river. For at that time the Most High performed signs for them, and stopped the channels of the river until they had crossed over. Through that region there was long way to go, a journey of a year and a half; and that country is called Arzareth."*

A sudden and dramatic change in the political climate is what gave rise to this new mass migration. Something unimaginable had occurred. In 634 B.C. the mighty Assyrians had fallen to another cruel Mesopotamian people, the Babylonians. The Babylonians ultimately acquired most of the Assyrian empire. But it was going to take time to consolidate their grip on all of those former holdings. This was the window that the Israelites needed.

Escape! Make a break for freedom! But to where? Should they go home to the land of Israel? That was not feasible, for the Babylonians would surely overtake them there. Then where should they go?

The natural northern boundary of empires in the Middle East was the large range of mountains called the Caucasus. Very high, not easily traversed, and spanning the distance from the Black Sea to the Caspian, this range separated the settled and populated regions to the south from the empty plains to the north. Prior to Christ, permanent towns did not exist in these steppes. Although many nomadic people traversed them, no one permanently dwelled there until later. During the period under discussion, the seventh century B.C., these prairies in what is now Russia and the Ukraine were analogous to a sea, with a number of ethnic groups passing through on their way to somewhere else. Even in recent centuries, the steppes have fostered empty nomadic lifestyles as illustrated in the Russian Cossack culture.

It was across the Caucasus Range, into the empty grasslands to the north, that the Israelites proposed to go. From their present location they would have to work their way northward through river valleys that approach the southern flanks of the mighty

Caucasus Range. Up the Euphrates, the Araxes, and the Rioni Rivers they had to travel. Then, these pioneering Israelites would have to wind their way through the narrow, snowy passes of the mountains, carrying all their worldly belongings. Yet depsite the fact they had women and children with them, they could not tarry, for at any time their former masters could give chase. Emerging from the north slopes of the Caucasus, they would be in the vast empty grasslands of what is now the Ukraine and Southern Russia. They would be free!

As previously stated in 2 Esdras 13:40-45, the Israelites were following the *"narrow passages of the Euphrates river."* They went northward, following the gorges of the Euphrates, gradually moving into *"Arzareth,"* a place *"where no human beings had ever lived."* It would take *"a year and a half"* to travel there

Caucusus Mountains

in a northward direction. Was Arzareth the empty grasslands north of the Caucasus range?

The historian Josephus, writing in the first century A.D., stated that the Israelite tribes of the northern kingdom were not lost to the world or absorbed amongst other people, but were found beyond the perimeters of the Roman Empire on the other side of the Euphrates river, i.e., to the north: *"So there are but two tribes in Asia and Europe subject to the Romans, while the ten tribes are beyond the Euphrates until now, and are an immense multitude, and not to be estimated by numbers" (Jewish Antiquities, Book 11; 5:2).* By *"Asia,"* Josephus, like other ancient writers, meant what we now call the Middle East. If the ten tribes he referred to were not in the portions of Europe and Asia controlled by the Romans, but were *"beyond the Euphrates,"* the most likely location is what was the region then called Scythia by some Greeks and Romans. Arzareth, therefore, was Scythia, or the plains of southern Russia and the Ukraine. Is there other evidence to support the idea that the deported Israelites went there?

Local tradition offers this. There is a mountain pass through the Caucasus that was widened into a modern highway in 1856. Called *Dariel Pass* today, the local inhabitants also call it the *Pass of Israel.*

Behistun Rock in modern Iran

On the northern slope is a prominent mountain adjacent to the pass the villagers call *Zion.* It received its name Dariel Pass because the Persian king Darius unsuccessfully attacked through the pass to avenge the death of Cyrus I, the founder of the Medo-Persian Empire. According to the great historian James Ussher, who quotes Herodotus and Valerius Maximus in his tome *The Annals of the World,* Cyrus *"was decapitated by Tomyris, the queen of the Scythians or Massagatae"* (p.119). Tamyris is the Greek form of *Tamar,* a common Israelite name. The ruins of a castle known by her name still can be observed guarding this pass.

Another remarkable bit of information are the gravestones from antiquity found in the Crimea, a peninsula in the Black Sea and an adjunct of ancient Scythia. According to Professor Chirolson of St. Petersburg, over seven hundred have been deciphered. One translation reads: *"I am Jehudi, the son of Moses, the son of Jehudi the Mighty, carried captive with other tribes of Israel by Shalmaneser . . . to Halah and Habor, to Gozan and to the Cheresonesus.*" This is plain and obvious evidence of the presence of Israelites in the region.

Sir Henry Rawlinson,
Archaeologist and Linguist
(1810-1895)

The *Jewish Encyclopedia* states this: *" . . . the Sacae, or Scythians, who, again, were the Lost Ten Tribes"* (Volume 12, p. 250). This is a plain assertion that the Israelites, subsequent to their deportation, moved into the region called Scythia, and indeed were called Scythians. Notice that the Sacae and the Scythians are used synonymously. Many scholars have determined they were one and the same people. They were the Israelites in a new region, now known by new names.

Sir Henry Rawlinson, the renowned archaeologist and linguist who deciphered the Behistun Rock, asserted the following: *"We have reasonable grounds for regarding the Gimirri, or Cimmerians, who first appeared on the confines of Assyria and Media in the seventh century B.C., and the Sacae of the Behistun Rock, nearly two centuries later, as identical with the Beth-Khumree of Samaria, or the Ten Tribes of the House of Israel . . ."* (*The Origins of the Nations*).

Much more solid evidence could be presented, but it becomes redundant. The summation of our story thus far is this: the Israelite tribes, after their deportation, made their way northward into what is now the steppes of Russia and the Ukraine along the shores of the Black and Caspian Seas, into a region called Scythia. They were numerous enough to interact with powerful neighbors to their south who called them variously Beth-Khumree (means House of Omri, after a notable king of the northern Israelites), Gimirri, Cimmerians, Scythians, Sacae, Massagatae or Gatae. But they had not yet reached what was to be their new homeland.

Then What Happened to the Twelve Tribes?

This need not be considered a mystery, for there is abundant evidence that identifies the Nordic race of northwest Europe as direct descendants of the aforementioned people found first in Greater Armenia, the region south of the Caucasus, and later in Scythia, the region north of the Caucasus. A few sources will demonstrate this, although many more could be cited.

The *Anglo-Saxon Chronicle* is one of the few major primary sources that narrate the events of pre-Norman Britain. Compiled in the ninth century, during the reign of Alfred the Great, it states the following about the original inhabitants of Britain: *"The first inhabitants were the Britons, who came from Armenia, and first peopled Britain southward. Then happened it, that the Picts came south from Scythia, with long ships . . ."* (p. 1). This remarkable piece of information reveals that the two dominant ethnic strains of the British race prior to the Romans came from the region exactly where the deported tribes of Israel had been. Is this coincidental?

Hardly, for the *Declaration of Arbroath* makes a very similar argument, but with the added usefulness of a timeline. Also known as the *Scottish Declaration of Independence*, this intriguing document was written to the Pope in 1320 A.D. to ask for his recognition of Scotland as a nation distinct from England and English ambitions. In describing their long history of independent activity, the Scots stated this: *"Most Holy Father and Lord, we know and from the chronicles and books of the ancients we find that among other famous nations our own, the Scots, has been graced with widespread renown. They journeyed from Greater Scythia by way of the Tyrrhenian Sea and the Pillars of Hercules, and dwelt for a long course of time in Spain among the most savage tribes, but nowhere could they be subdued by any race, however barbarous. Thence they came, twelve hundred years after the people of Israel crossed* the Red Sea, to their home in the west where they still live today." Not only does this place the ancestors of the Scots in Scythia, but it also indicates that this migration was completed from Scythia to Scotland via Spain no later than 291 B.C., for the Israelites crossed the Red Sea in 1491 B.C. Although the elapsed time in Spain is unstated, the movement out of Scythia is identical to the period when a broad movement of Scythians (i.e. Israelites) westward into Europe was

Scottish monument commemorating the Declaration of Arbroath, A.D. 1220

occurring, as will be shortly discussed. And although the document does not state that the Scots are directly descended from the Israelites, we can deduce that they must be. They were in Scythia when the Israelites were there. Furthermore, why else would the Scots mention such a landmark event as Israel's crossing of the Red Sea if they were not Israelites?

Another document of antiquity, *The Brut* or *The Chronicles of the Kings of Briton*, has a remarkable comment regarding a Scottish chief name Bathlome, a commander of thirty ships who was speaking to Gwrganr, an ancient king of Britain: *"This chief related to the king the whole of their adventures, from the time they had been driven from Israel their original country, and the manner and circumstances in which their ancestors dwelt in a retired part of Spain, near Eirnia, from whence the Spaniards drove them to sea to seek another abode"* (p. 60). This statement corroborates the whole idea that the Scots are Israelites as inferred in the *Arbroath Declaration.*

Next we shall consider Sharon Turner's *The History of the Anglo-Saxons from the Earliest Period to the Norman Conquest.* Originally published between 1799 and 1805, it has long been considered the definitive work regarding the early history of Europe. Continuously referring to ancient writers whenever possible, Turner elaborates in painstaking detail the movement of the Saxon race out of Greater Armenia and Scythia into western Europe.

With respect to the origins of the Saxon race, consider Turner's comments: *"The Anglo-Saxons, the lowland Scotch, Normans, Danes, Norwegians, Swedes, Germans, Dutch, Belgians,*

Lombards, and Franks have all sprung from that great fountain of the human race, which we have distinguished by the terms, Scythian, German, or Goth . . . The first appearance of the Scythian tribes in Europe may be placed, according to Strabo and Homer, about the eighth, or according to Herodotus, in the seventh century before the Christian era . . . Their general appellation among themselves was

Sharon Turner, English historian (1768-1847)

Scoloti, but the Greeks called them Scythians, Scuthoi, or Nomades . . . the Sakai, the Massagatai drew their origin from them" (Turner, *History of the Anglo-Saxons,* p. 57).

As can be seen, the timeline that Turner suggests is exactly when the northern tribes of Israel were moving out of Palestine into Greater Armenia and Scythia. Notice also the names he identifies them as: Scythians, Sakai, Massagatai, and interestingly,

Scoloti, a name remarkably similar to Scots. Coincidental? Surely not. He continues and identifies the geography more precisely: *"The emigrating Scythians crossed the Araxes, passed out of Asia . . . and suddenly appeared in Europe, in the seventh century before the Christian era"* (ibid., p.58). The Araxes River is a major stream in Greater Armenia, just south of the Caucasus Mountains in what is now the country of Turkey, only a short distance north from the biblical locations of Halah, Habor, and Gozan.

Concerning the etymology of names, Turner states: *"It would be impertinent to the great subject of this history to engage in a minuter discussion of the Scythian tribes. They have become better known to us, in recent periods, under the name of Getae and Goths, the most celebrated of their branches . . . The Saxons were a German or Teutonic, that is, a Gothic or Scythian tribe; and of the various Scythian nations which have been recorded, the Sakai, or Sacae, are the people from whom the descent of the Saxons may be inferred, with the least violation of probability. Sakai-suna, or the sons of the Sakai, abbreviated into Saksun, which is the same sound as Saxon, seems a reasonable etymology of the word Saxon"* (ibid., pp. 58-59). As one can see, despite Turner's passing reference to brevity, he continued to elaborate regarding the Gothic and Saxon tribes of western Europe as the direct descendants of the Scythians or Sacae from Greater Armenia and Scythia in the seventh and eighth centuries before Christ.

The Twelve Tribes Are Caucasian Europeans

As a final observation, consider what the Huguenot scholar and refugee Dr. Jacques Abbadie had to say on the topic in 1723: *"Unless the ten tribes of Israel are flown into the air, or sunk into the earth, they must be those ten Gothic tribes that entered Europe in the fifth century B.C. . . . and founded the ten nations of modern Europe"* (*The Triumph of Providence* as taken from the *National Message*, 6/1957, p. 188).

More historical evidence could be cited, but the summation of the matter is this: the twelve tribes of Israel were the parent stock of most of the modern nations of Europe.

To insist that the Lost Tribes of Israel were completely absorbed by other nations is simply at odds with historical and archaeological evidence. Other claims regarding the identity of the lost tribes, connecting them to the Japanese, the Meso-Americans, or African tribes, is not merely inaccurate, but either dishonest or incompetent. If you are a person descended from the Anglo-Saxon race of nations of Europe, you have a fabulous inheritance that resides in your genes. Do not let it slip away from you!

2

Linguistic and Archaeological Evidence: Linking the Ancient Hebrews to Europe and America

*"Those we call the ancients
were really new in everything."*
–Blaise Pascal

For quite some time, it has been generally assumed that the Western Christian nations of Europe and North America have little connection to the Hebrews of the Old Testament. In terms of their religious heritage, these Caucasian Christian peoples were assumed to have simply adopted the Scriptures of the ancient Israelites and were "grafted in" to a spiritual church body during and subsequent to the New Testament era.

The greater truth is gradually being revealed by linguistics, archaeology, and historic records. More and more solid evidence is proving that there is a genetic link between ancient Hebrews and the Caucasian peoples of Western Europe. Exploration, trade, and colonization with the Western nations of Europe and even further afield are being clearly revealed. The evidence shows that Hebrew colonists left the Middle East during the Israelite captivity in Egypt and settled in various parts of Europe including Greece,

Italy, Spain, Ireland, and England. Much later, during the heady days of glory and power under David and Solomon, extensive trade routes were established to these aforementioned and other regions which grew into prosperous colonies. A close investigation of these links will prove fascinating.

Linguistic Evidence

One of the most durable connecting links indicating genetic descent is language. Languages are constantly changing and shifting, yet these numerous incremental alterations do not erase certain recognizable bases, roots, suffixes, etc. of common words. The modern languages of Western Europe are descended from the ancient Hebrew tongue. This is the expert opinion of a number of linguistic scholars who have reached this conclusion independent of one another.

Dr. Louis Hjelmslev (1899-1965), founder of the Copenhagen School of Linguistics.

The founder of modern anthropology, Dr. James Prichard, published a study in 1857 entitled *Eastern Origin of Celtic Nations*. He determined that the Celtic language *"forms an intermediate link between [the Indo-European] and the Semitic, or perhaps indicates a state of transition" (p. 349)*. He further states that *". . . even cautious investigators have not only given a list of Semitic elements in the Keltic, but have made the Keltic specially Semitic."* That genetic descent is thus probable is verified by Prichard when he comments, *"A common language is prima facie evidence in favor of a common lineage" (p. 380)*.

Dr. William Worrell, a professor of Semitics at University of Michigan, stated this in his 1927 book *A Study of Races in the*

Ancient Near East: *"In the British Isles certain syntactic phenomena of insular Celtic speech have led to the inference that in this region languages were spoken which had some relation, however remote, to the Hamitic-Semitic family"* (p. 46). He then goes to great lengths to show how ancient Egyptian and Hebrew are connected to the Celtic tongue.

Danish scholar Dr. Louis Hjelmslev comments in 1960 in his book *Language: An Introduction*, referring to the work of a colleague: *"A genetic relationship between Indo-European and Hamito-Semitic [i.e., Egyptian-Hebrew] was demonstrated in detail . . ."* (p. 79). Since that time, Danish scholars have proposed eliminating the separate language categories of Semitic and Indo-European, combining them in a new category called Nostratic, meaning "our own countryman."

In 1982, Dr. Terry Blodgett, an American linguist, received considerable attention for his doctoral dissertation *Similarities in Germanic and Hebrew.* He declares his research *"has traced various tribes of Israel into Europe."* A newspaper review of his work summarizes nicely: *"Recent discoveries concerning the Germanic languages suggest there must have been extensive Hebrew influence in Europe, especially in England, Holland, Scandinavia, and Germany during the last seven centuries of the pre-Christian era [700 B.C. to Christ]"* (Salt Lake

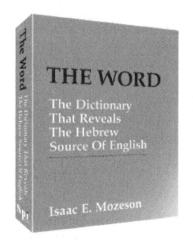

THE WORD

The Dictionary
That Reveals
The Hebrew
Source Of English

Isaac E. Mozeson

Tribune, October 21, 1982) This influence would be a result of the dispersion of the Northern ten tribes of Israel after they were taken into captivity by the Assyrians in 721 B.C.

Dr. Isaac Mozeson, a Hebrew language scholar at Yeshiva University, published in 1989 a massive volume entitled *The Word,*

The Dictionary that Reveals the Hebrew Source of English.
He demonstrates that over 5,000 common English words are of
Semitic origin. He concludes by declaring *"that English and
Hebrew are profoundly connected."*

It is a reasonable and safe assumption that linguistics prove
that there is a clear and definite genetic link between the ancient
Hebrews and the peoples of modern European extraction. How
did this occur? What are the historical events that made such
profound connections? Why is it not more well-known?

The Maritime Influence
of David and Solomon

The sea travels and trading influences of the ancient Phoenicians
have been documented. What has not been documented is the
fact that the Israelites and the Phoenicians were inextricable
partners in these adventures, much like the Danes, Norwegians,
and Swedes were a trio of seafaring adventurers during their own
Viking era.

In *The Bible Handbook* Dr. Joseph Angus states,
*". . . The Hebrew language was the common tongue of
Canaan and Phoenicia is generally admitted."* The well known
archaeologist George Rawlinson had this to say regarding the
Hebrew alphabet: *". . . This alphabet is that which has been
commonly called Phoenecian, because the Greeks ascribed its
invention to that people. It is, like the Hebrew, an alphabet
of twenty-two letters."*

In addition to sharing an alphabet and language that differed
only in dialect, the Hebrews and Phoenecians shared a common
racial origin, both claiming descent from Shem. The Phoenicians
and Hebrews had a common enemy, the Philistines. The fact
that Elijah stayed at length with a Phoenecian widow in Zarephath
(1 Kings 17:9-16) indicates a close and comfortable relationship
between the two peoples. The alliance between King David of

Israel and King Hiram of Tyre is well known. Hiram supplied David with lumber and skilled craftsman to build his palace, while David provided grain. The military land forces of David and Solomon were without challengers in the Middle East, and the commercial and naval power of Tyre, the leading Phoenecian city-state, created a formidable alliance. During this period, Assyria and Egypt were quiescent, and Israel dominated the entire Middle East, holding many nations as vassals: Edom, Moab, Ammon, and Syria.

Solomon was determined to execise maritime power as well. Working with the Phoenicians, he built a fleet of ships in Eziongeber, at the north tip of the Red Sea. Hiram sent special naval experts to train Solomon's own sailors (1 Kings 9:26-27). It was

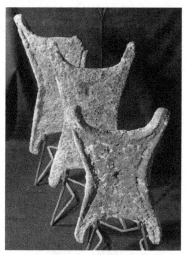

Copper "oxhide" Ingots from Ezion-geber

here, at this southern port of Israel, that massive copper smelters have been excavated by archaeologists and ascribed to the reign of Solomon. To this port, huge quantities of copper ore were shipped for smelting before being brought overland to Jerusalem. From where did this ore come? One intriguing possibility is that it was mined in North America and then brought across the Atlantic, then the Mediterranean, and finally through an ancient canal where the modern Suez Canal is now. This may seem far-fetched to an initiate of ancient history, but certain facts make it a reasonable possibility.

Archeologists now know that ships as heavy as 600 tons regularly plyed the waters of the Indian and Atlantic oceans in ancient times. This is far larger than Columbus's largest ship in 1492. The naval technology existed for trans-Atlantic voyages.

One of Solomon's wives was the daughter of the Egyptian Pharoah, meaning he would likely have had access to the canal connecting the Red and Mediterranean Seas. Sesostris III of Egypt is credited as the first to open and maintain a Nile-Red Sea waterway, thus linking it to the Mediterranean, probably around 1400 B.C. Parts of the channel of this canal were still visible in the Wadi Tumilat and were followed by the engineers as they laid out the modern Suez Canal.

Remarkably, there is strong evidence that Hebrews and Phoenicians traveled across the Atlantic to trade for copper and other resources. Several sites have been discovered in the Lake Superior region of North America where considerable copper mining occurred. The dates associated with these sites are about 1000 B.C. Dr. Barry Fell, a professor emeritus of Harvard University, cites evidence that indicates the Phoenicians had regular ports of call on the Maine coast. He states this in his book *America B.C.*:

Ten Commandments in ancient Hebrew Script near Los Lunas, New Mexico.

"these inscriptions, therefore, suggest that organized international maritime commerce was well established in the late Bronze Age, that North American ports were listed on the sailing timetables of the overseas vessels of the principal Phoenician shipping companies, and that the same information was circulated to customers in America" (p. 100-101).
Further evidence that the Phoenicians were in America in ancient times was found in a site known as Mystery Hill in New Hampshire. Here are found ruins of shrines dedicated to the Phoenician and Canaanite god Baal.

Is it possible that ancient Hebrews were present in North America during this same period? It is more than possible—it is likely. Near Los Lunas, New Mexico, a set of ancient Hebrew inscriptions have been found of the Ten Commandments from Exodus 20. Additionally, inscriptions in the Hebrew/Phoenician language have been found in various locations all across North America referring to the *"ships of Tarshish."* These discoveries in West Virginia, Rhode Island, Ohio, and elsewhere are plainly talking about one of two places called Tarshish in ancient times, both of Hebrew origin. The most likely location of ancient Tarshish is Spain. Long associated with the Phoenician trading empire, we know that Israelites were also present in Spain. It was from Spain (Tarshish)

Davenport Stele, describing how to calculate the new year.

that Solomon sent fleets down the coast of Africa and brought back gold, silver, ivory, apes, and peacocks (1 Kings 10:22).

A remarkable stone stele was found near Davenport, Iowa in 1874. It languished in obscurity for nearly a century because imbedded on it were inscriptions in three languages, all thought to be of Mediterranean origin, and thus an enigma for historians and archaeologists. The three languages were Egyptian, Iberian-Punic, and Libyan. The latter two are definitely Semitic and connect this monument to the ancient Hebrews. Iberian-Punic was a Semitic language spoken in Spain and the northern coast of Africa around Carthage. On this topic Dr. Barry Fell stated, *"The Punic language can be read without difficulty, as it is similar to ancient Hebrew."* Both Carthage and the coast of ancient

Libya were colonized by Hebrew/Phoenician settlers beginning during the reign of Solomon and continuing subsequent to the breakup of Israel after Solomon's death. After the revolt of the northern ten tribes, the maritime empire that was allied with the

A Hebrew inscription found in
Bat Creek, Tennessee. It reads, "for Judea."

Phoenicians was dominated by the wealthier and more populous Northern Kingdom of Israel. In particular, the tribes of Zebulon, Asher, Naphtali, and Dan continued to prosper because of their proximity adjacent to the Phoenician city-states and the Mediterranean coastline. As the population of the Northern Kingdom grew, colonizers set out to the West. It was during this period that Carthage was founded on the north coast of Africa, Cadiz in Spain, as well as other settlements along the shores of the Mediterranean. Interestingly, the ancient name of *Cadiz* is *Gades*, indicating a probable link to the northern tribe of Gad. Also, the Spanish city of *Saragosa* is possibly a cognate of *Zarah*, a prominent man in the tribe of Judah.

Another intriguing inscription was found in 1889 in a burial mound at Bat Creek, Tennessee. This inscription is in Hebrew and is dated even earlier, about 1600 B.C. (*America B.C.*, p. 318). Along with the inscription were found brass bracelets likely to be of Roman origin since the ratio of lead to zinc in the brass is the same as Roman brass of the first century A.D.

All of this archaeological evidence points to a simple fact: old world people found their way to North America in ancient times. This included Israelites who emigrated from Palestine to distant places in reasonably large numbers prior to the destruction of the northern state of Israel in 721 B.C. Much of this emigration was to several regions in Western Europe, and some degree of visitation was to locations as far away as North America.

Very Early Links to Europe

There is clear evidence linking ancient Israelites to the British Isles and other locations in Western Europe. For example, the sixteenth century English historian William Camden wrote, *"The merchants of Asher worked the tin mines of Cornwall, not as slaves, but as masters and exporters" (Britannia, p. 231).* Another British historian, Edward Creasy, wrote in the nineteenth century, *"The British mines mainly supplied the glorious adornment of Solomon's Temple."*

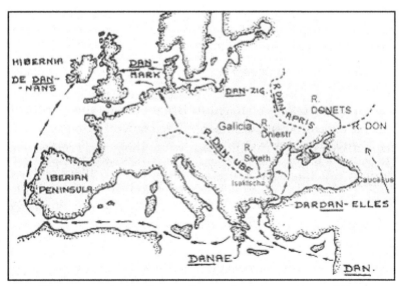

This map shows the routes and place-names of the Danites that left the land of Israel prior to 721 B.C. as part of a general migration of Israelites into Western Europe.

There are clues that indicate that a portion (not all) of the tribe of Dan separated politically from the rest of the thirteen tribes of Israel very early in their history, no later than the period under the judges. Judges 5:17 states that Dan did *"remain in ships."* Ezekiel 27, in listing the various nations that did business with Tyre, gave Dan its own identity separate from Israel and Judah. It is known that the Greeks had considerable contact with a Mediterranean seafaring people known as Danaans, or Danuana as early as 1200 B.C. Were these from the Hebrew tribe of Dan? It seems they were. Archaeologist Yigael Yadin made the following comment in *Biblical Archaeology Review:* *". . . The Danites were originally not members of the Israelite confederation . . . They seem, rather, to have been connected with a group of the Sea Peoples called Danuna or Denyen in Egyptian sources, and known to the Greeks as the Danaoi."* The Danaans are known to have sailed and settled in a number of far flung locations throughout Europe including the Ukraine, Spain, Ireland, Britain, and, not surprisingly, Denmark. Part of a general migration westward into the regions of Western Europe, their trade included tin from Cornwall, amber from the Baltic Sea coasts, and furs from Scandinavia.

Britain had long been a regular port of call for Phoenicians and Hebrews. Thus, it comes as no surprise when we discover that Israelite settlers migrated to Britain during this period of Israelite expansion overseas. Concerning the Welsh connection to ancient Israel, John Hardin Allen wrote this: *". . . the people of Wales call themselves, in ancient Welsh, 'Bryth y Brithan', or 'Briths of Briton,' which means 'The Covenanters' of the 'land of Covenant.' The first form of this phrase is almost vernacular Hebrew"* (*Judah's Sceptre and Joseph's Birthright, p. 121*).

When the northern kingdom of Israel began to collapse in the face of the growing Assyrian behemoth, many Israelites chose to emigrate to these already established overseas colonies. A series of invasions over a span of many years, culminating in 721 B.C. and the capture of Samaria after a three-year siege, sent thousands of Israelites scattering to Carthage, Spain, Ireland, and Wales. Those that settled in the British Isles and the west coast of France formed the nucleus of Celtic culture and society that preceded later Israelite migrations into Europe by several hundred years.

What this chapter has outlined is only a modest sketch of the documentation connecting the Caucasian people of Western European descent to the ancient Israelites. We have briefly focused on the time period prior to the dissolution of the Northern Kingdom in 721 B.C. Large quantities of material also exist that discuss the mass migration of the ten tribes subsequent to the dispersion of 721 B.C., as was discussed in the previous chapter. The facts of history, archaeology, and linguistics speak for themselves to those who are open-minded enough to consider them. The Caucasians of Western Europe are the direct descendants of the ancient Israelites.

3

The Antiquity of the Anglo-Israel Thesis

"The high minded man must care more for the truth than for what people think."
–Aristotle

Many are the critics who denounce the idea that Caucasians have a genetic connection to ancient Israelites of the Old Testament. Suggesting that White people of European extraction are the descendants of the lost ten tribes often invites scorn and reproofs from mainstream theologians and academics. Yet, when asked to offer proof that such a thesis is erroneous, the evidence presented is always brief and shallow and quickly deteriorates into name calling and asserting that anyone who might adhere to such a belief is a "kook" or a "racist."

By itself, the fact that many mainstream academics ridicule this idea does not make it false. Mainstream academics scoffed at Copernicus and persecuted Galileo when these great minds suggested that the sun was the center of the solar system rather than the earth. Mainstream academics were wrong. For the last eighty years mainstream academics have told us the solar system had nine planets; now, Pluto is no longer a planet, so there are just eight planets. Evidently mainstream academics were wrong.

More recently, mainstream academics are busy mocking anyone who believes the earth was designed with a self-adjusting climatic feedback system, insisting instead that man-made global warming is about to destroy the planet. Even as you read this, overwhelming evidence is piling up that the mainstream academics are wrong.

Truth is revealed when the merits of an argument are allowed open and free examination. Too often, mainstream academics, eager to protect their turf for political and economic reasons, will suppress ideas that make them uncomfortable. That is the case regarding the Anglo-Israel thesis.

One of the key points of contention in this debate is the origin of the thesis. Who originated the thought that Caucasians of northwest Europe are the genetic descendants of the lost ten tribes of Israel?

Mainstream academics posit that an eccentric English gentleman, Richard Brothers (1757-1824), developed the notion rather recently, only about two hundred years ago. Brothers also claimed that he himself was to inherit the throne of England and went on to be incarcerated in an insane asylum for several years on the grounds of possible treason. He thus gives the appearance of being non-credible. If he were the founder of the Anglo-Israel thesis, it did indeed have a rocky start. Thus, to discredit the idea at its very source, mainstream academics repeatedly assert that Richard Brothers was its true originator and prime advocate.

It is the purpose of this chapter to demonstrate that many other writers and documents pre-date Richard Brothers in the assertion of the Anglo-Israel thesis. Indeed, they precede him, not by just a few decades, but by wide expanses of time. However, proving that this idea is an old one does not necessarily make it true. Additional essays by this author and other skilled expositors of the Bible and history offer the necessary evidence to build its veracity. Yet proving the antiquity of the Anglo-Israel message does demonstrate a strong measure of credibility; if many writers from varied locations and over long time periods believed that it is true, surely it is an idea that deserves an unbiased examination and should not be lightly dismissed to the realm of "kooks."

Let us travel backward in time. Beginning with the period of history immediately preceding Richard Brothers (1757-1824), let us work our way ever deeper into antiquity and pursue this thesis of whether people from Europe are the descendants of the ancient Israelites. How far back in time does this idea go?

The English Puritans

In the English-speaking world, Puritan thinkers dominated the seventeenth and eighteenth centuries. From a distance of over three centuries, we tend to generalize the Puritan movement and place them all in a box. You know the image: they only dressed in black, never smiled, carried gigantic Bibles, hated fun, and spent a lot of time falsely accusing old ladies of being witches. In point of fact, with the exception of carrying large Bibles (all Bibles were large in those days), every one of those popular images is a mischaracterization. While it is not our purpose to explore every facet of what Puritans

Cotton Mather (1663-1728) a prolific writer and minister, knew that the New England Puritans were Israelites.

were like, let it be stated for the record that the term *Puritan* became a catchall term for any Englishman who had any dissatisfaction with the state church, the Church of England. Beyond that, they truly comprised a broad array of theological ideas. Englishmen on both sides of the Atlantic were caught up in deep exploration of the Bible and their own role in God's unfolding plan of history. Puritans did not always agree with each other; but despite their differences, their writings almost always reflect sensible, cogent arguments based on honest readings of Scripture. Some of these Puritans believed that they were descended from the tribes of ancient Israel. And to prove it, consider the following quotations by these prominent Puritans divines:

Cotton Mather, the author of more than 450 works and an American Puritan minister, wrote *The Ecclesiastical History of New England* in 1702 about the Puritans who emigrated from England to America. In this work are sundry passages revealing his belief that they were the offspring of biblical Israel:

John Milton, the most talented Engish writer of the seventeenth century, identified the English as sons of Sacae, or Israelites.

· *". . . our hastening voyage unto the history of a new English-Israel."*

· *"These good people were now satisfyed, they had as plain a command of Heaven to attempt a removal, as ever their father Abraham had for his leaving Chaldean territories."*

· *"Among these passengers were divers worthy and useful men, who were come to seek the welfare of this little Israel."*

· *"To give them such hearts as were in Abraham and others of their famous and faithful fathers."*

· *"An introduction unto this piece of New English history; that when some ecclesiastical oppressions drive a colony of the truest Israelites into the remoter parts of the world . . ."*

· *"The enemies of New England owed the wondrous disasters and confusions that still followed them as much to the prayers of this true Israelite as to perhaps any one occasion."*

· *"Here lies Nathanael, True offspring of God's Israel."*

John Milton was the author of *Paradise Lost* and the seventeenth century's most celebrated English poet and writer. An enormously skilled wordsmith and a man of unexcelled brilliance in all things literary, Milton believed that the Saxon tribes that settled England were direct descendants of the Israelites. In his work *The History of Britain*, published in 1670, he wrote this of the Saxons: *"They were a people thought by good writers to be descendants of the Sacae, a kind of Scythians in the north of Asia, thence called Sacasons, or sons of Sacae, who with a flood of other northern nations came into Europe, toward the declining of the Roman empire."*

Nathaniel Morton, a New England Puritan of some reputation and the court secretary for New Plymouth, wrote the following statements in 1669 in his book *New England's Memorial*:

· *"That especially the seed of Abraham his servant, and the children of Jacob his chosen, may remember his marvelous works in the beginning and progress of the planting of New England."*

· *"God . . . brought to nought their wicked devices [the American Indians] . . . until he had accomplished the freedom of his Israel, by the overthrow of his and their enemies."*

John Bunyan, author of *Pilgrim's Progress*, "actually fancied himself an Israelite."

Edward Johnson was a historian of the Puritan movement in England and New England. He often spoke of the English people as literal Israelites. In his book *Johnson's Wonder-Working Providences of Sion's Savior in New England*, published in 1630, he wrote the following, referring to the Puritan settlers coming from England:

· *"The Lambe is preparing his Bride . . . yee the ancient Beloved of Christ, whom he of old led by the hand from Egypt to Canaan through that great and terrible wilderness."*

· *"You the Seed of Israel both lesse and more, the rattling of your dead bones together is at hand, Sinewes, Flesh and Life: at the Word of Christ it comes."*

John Bunyan (1628-1688), the author of *Pilgrim's Progress* (written from a prison cell), believed he was an Israelite, according to the Jewish Rabbi Louis Finkelstein who analyzed his works: *"Bunyan actually fancied himself an Israelite . . ." (The Jews: Their History, p. 86).*

Enlightenment and Reformation Era Scholars

The eighteenth century was dominated by a broad intellectual movement known as the Enlightenment, a time of lofty idealistic pursuits. It is often mischaracterized as being overtly hostile to Christianity. While some prominent writers were, such generalization is inaccurate. Some scoffed at the Christian faith; others defended it.

Preceding the Enlightenment, the Protestant Reformation was a 250-year period of religious revival and tumult across Europe that began earlier and then ran more or less contemporaneously to the Puritan movement in England. There were a variety of theological opinions publicly vented during this exciting time; but again, like the Puritans in England, all viewpoints were grounded in literal and honest readings of Scripture, even if the interpretations were not always identical. Among the ideas voiced was the theme that God was actively working among His Israelite people, who were to be found in the nations of Europe. Consider the following:

Olof von Dalin, an eighteenth century Swedish historian, believed that the ancient Finns, Lapps, and Estonians sprang from the Neuri, who were ultimately descended from the ancient Israelites. He wrote this: *". . . the Neuri seem to be remnants of the Ten Tribes of Israel which Shalmaneser, king of Assyria, brought as captives out of Caanan . . . [when one realizes that] the language of the ancient Finns, Lapps, and Estonians is similar to Hebrew and even that this people in ancient times reckoned their year's beginning from the first of March, and Saturday as their Sabbath, then one sees that the Neuri in all probability had this origin"* (*Svearikes Historia, Volume 1,* 1747, p. 54-55).

Olof Rudbeck the Younger (1660-1740) was a Swedish noble who asserted that the Sami language of Lapland was closely connected to Hebrew. He argued that this was clear proof of genetic descent.

Johannes Jacobi Eurenius (1688-1751), a Swedish dean and pastor in Angermanland and Torsaker, was an advocate that the Hebrews had many connections to Western European regions in ancient times. He believed the Swedes, along with the other

A young Finnish woman in traditonal dress. Swedish scholars have connected the Finnish language, along with the Lapp and Estonian, as derived from ancient Hebrew.

Europeans, were Israelites. Among his other arguments, he observed a linguistic relationship and stated this in his book *Atlantica Orientalis*: *"Furthermore, the language which we have kept confirms that our ancestors have sprung from the fled Israelites and Scythians, since we have an extraordinary mixture of the languages through which the Israelites stayed during their exodus out of the Orient and wandered through."*

Dr. Jacques Abaddie, a French Huguenot who was forced to flee France, eventually settled in Ireland and became the Dean of Killaloe. In his four-volume work *Le Triomphe de la Providence et de la Religion*, published in 1723, he wrote this: *"Certainly, unless the Ten Tribes have flown into the air, or been plunged to the earth's centre, they must be sought in that part of the North . . . namely among the Iberians, Armenians, and Scythians; for that was the place of their dispersion—the wilderness where*

William Tyndale (1492-1536)
English Bible translator

God caused them to dwell in tents . . . Perhaps if the subject was carefully examined, it would be found that the nations who in the fifth age made irruption into the Roman Empire, and who Procopius reduced to ten in number, were in effect the Ten Tribes who made their home in Europe . . . Everything fortifies this conjecture; the extraordinary multiplication of this people, marked so precisely by the prophets, the number of the tribes, the custom of those nations to dwell in tents, according to the oracles, and many other usages of the Scythians similar to those of the children of Israel."

Henry Spelman (1562-1641), a noted English scholar of church history, was the author of *Concilia Ecclesiastica Orbis Britannici* and *Glossarium Archaiologicum*. According to his eighteenth century biographer Peter Suhm, Spelman believed that the Danes, Norwegians, and Goths were Hebrews and that the Danes were in particular of the tribe of Dan.

Adriian van der Schriek was a prominent Dutch scholar who published a book in 1614, *Troost Mijn Volk*. In the subtitle he stated, *"The Netherlanders with the Gauls and Germans together in the earliest times were called Celts, who came out of the Hebrews."*

Pierre Le Loyer, a French Huguenot, wrote this in 1590 in his work *The Ten Lost Tribes Found*: *"The Israelites came to and founded the English Isles."*

William Tyndale, the renowned English Bible translator, like Johannes Eureius, observed a surprisingly close affinity between Hebrew and the Germanic languages of northwest Europe (German, Dutch, Swedish, Norwegian, Danish, and English). In 1530 he famously stated, *"The properties of the Hebrew tongue agreeth a thousand times more with the English than with the Latin. The manner of speaking is both one; so that in a thousand places thou needest not but to translate it into English, word for word . . ."*

Medieval European Sources

The Declaration of Arbroath, one of the most remarkable medieval documents, strongly infers that the Scots were descendants of the Israelites of old. Although discussed in chapter one, it is worth revisiting here. Also known as the *Scottish Declaration of Independence*, this intriguing document was addressed to the Pope in the 1320 to ask for his recognition of Scotland as a nation distinct from England and

The Declaration of Arbroath

English ambitions. Drafted by Bernard de Linton, the Abbot of Aberbrothick and the Chancellor of Scotland, it was signed by twenty-five Scottish nobles and Robert the Bruce, the King of Scotland. This English translation of the original Latin states: *"Most Holy Father and Lord, we know and from the chronicles and books of the ancients we find that among other famous nations our own, the Scots, has been graced with widespread renown. They journeyed from Greater Scythia by way of the Mediterranean Sea and the Pillars of Hercules, and dwelt for a long course of time in Spain amoung the most savage tribes, but nowhere could they be subdued by any race, however barbarous. Thence they came, twelve hundred years after the people of Israel crossed the Red Sea, to their home in the West where they still live today."* This document places the ancestors of the Scots in Scythia in precisely the period of time when the ten tribes of Israel

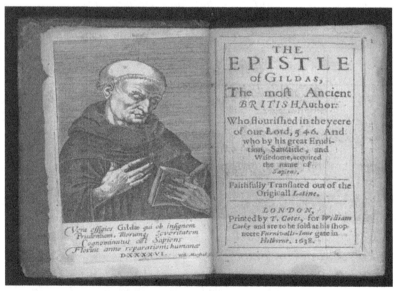

Gildas, British historian (A.D. 500-570)

were moving westward. Furthermore, by mentioning the landmark event of the crossing of the Red Sea, it marks them as having a unique connection to the ancient Israelites of Old Testament fame, a relationship that implies genetic descent.

Gildas, an early British historian and cleric writing in the sixth century A.D., showed his distress at the invasions of the Saxons and wrote that these events were taking place *"to the end that our Lord might try this land after his accustomed manner these His Israelites whether they loved him or not"* (*De Excidio et Conquestu Britanniae*).

Prior to Gildas there exists a body of evidence in the British Isles that predates the coming of the Romans. Although these documents do not rise to the standard historians prefer and skeptics will dismiss as legendary, they are nonetheless worth noting because they are contemporary to the events under consideration. They are thus the earliest documents that exist that can be considered as possible eyewitnesses to the movement of Israelitish people from the Near East to northwest Europe.

One of these is particularly plain. In *The Brut*, or the *Chronicles of the Kings of Briton*, a Scottish chief named Bathlome, a commander of *"thirty ships,"* spoke to a king named Gwrganr. In this conversation, *"This chief related to king the whole of their adventures, from the time they had been driven from Israel, their original country, and the manner and circumstances in which their ancestors dwelt in a retired part of Spain, near Eirnia, from whence Spaniards drove them to sea to seek another abode."*

Witnesses from the Classical World

Josephus was the premier Judean historian of the first century A.D. An early supporter of the Judean uprising in A.D. 70, he was captured and then paroled by the Romans after the uprising was defeated. He went on to write a detailed and voluminous account of the history of the Hebrews up to his own time. He identified the ten tribes of Israel in existence beyond the reaches of the Roman Empire in southwest Asia. This was exactly where they would have been after their escape from the Assyrian captivity on their slow but steady migration westward into Europe. In Book

2, chapter 5. 2:133, he wrote this: *"So there are but two tribes in Asia and Europe subject to the Romans, while the ten tribes are beyond the Euphrates until now, and are an immense multitude, and not to be estimated by numbers."*

Spartans in the *Apocrypha*, in about 200 BC, state quite clearly that they were Israelites: *"King Arius of the Spartans, to the high priest Onias, greetings. It has been found in writing concerning the Spartans and the Jews that they are brothers and are of the family of Abraham" (1 Maccabees 12:20-21)*. The Apocrypha is a reliable source, well documented and considered of nearly equal value as the sixty-six canonized books of the Bible. Indeed, the original edition of the King James Bible included the *Apocrypha* as did many other Bibles of the Reformation era. For the *Apocrypha* to identify such a notable collection of people as the Greek Spartans as being relatives to the people of Judea is almost unimpeachable evidence that it is true.

To Conclude

Having seen with your own eyes the testimony of prominent men in history that adopted the thesis that Caucasians are Israelites, you are in a position to know that Richard Brothers did not launch this idea. As is obvious, it is a thesis with a long history into antiquity. Just because it is politically incorrect does not make it false. Indeed, the intellectual tyranny of our own time in the media and academia that tries so hard to scorn this idea without ever looking at the facts is prima facie evidence that this is a potent idea worthy of honest examination.

Are you brave and honest enough to read more about this idea and see if history and Scripture offer evidence of its truth? Or, will you plug your eyes and ears and return to the screamers of political correctness who insist that supporters of this idea are nothing more than "kooks" and "racists," all the while providing no thoughtful rebuttal based on evidence? Could it be that there is no thoughtful, evidence-based rebuttal?

4

New Testament Evidence: Greeks, Romans, and Gauls Are Israelites by Other Names

"What's in a name? That which we call a rose by any other name would smell just as sweet."
–William Shakespeare, *Romeo and Juliet*

As has been shown in the previous chapters, there are good reasons to conclude that Caucasian Europeans are the physical, literal descendants of the tribes of Israel. Many Israelites had been taken into captivity by the Assyrians in the eighth century B.C. and subsequently made their way to Europe. Others had migrated there in even earlier times. There is solid evidence from ancient historical documents and archaeology that proves these claims. Excellent linguistic evidence demonstrates this connection. This has already been reviewed.

But setting all such evidence aside, if the only source of information one possessed were the New Testament, the same conclusion must be drawn. There are enough New Testament clues that the Israelites of old are the direct ancestors of the people of Europe that any objective analysis will allow no other verdict. The key to observing this truth, so often overlooked, is to simply read the New Testament in the plainest sense, without assuming that things literal must be somehow "spiritualized." It is commonly assumed that the idea of "spiritual Israel" is the pre-eminent theme of the New Testament. But that term appears nowhere in the text of the entire Bible, nor is that idea taught by any writer of the New Testament. Indeed, the concept is completely unnecessary if one can correctly identify the descendants of the tribes of Israel in the New Testament era.

Let the reader now peruse the New Testament and witness for himself the evidence showing that the two great European peoples profiled in the New Testament, the Romans and the Greeks, were genetic Israelites in the most literal sense.

As an appetizer, consider the words in Matthew's Gospel, when Jesus stated, *"I am not sent but unto the lost sheep of the house of Israel" (Matthew 15:24).* Later, Jesus reminded His twelve disciples that if they were faithful, they would receive an outstanding commission in His new order: *"Verily I say unto you, that ye which have followed me, in the regeneration when the Son of man shall sit in the throne of his glory, ye also shall sit upon twelve thrones, judging the twelve tribes of Israel" (Matthew 19:28).* So you see, Jesus was quite interested in the people of Israel; indeed, He was concerned with no others.

Consider now Paul, the apostle to the Greeks and Romans, nations which many assume to have been non-Israelite. Is this right? Or could it be that Paul went to genetic Israelites who had, many hundreds of years before, come to be known by other names? Is this possible?

In the book of Acts, Paul finds himself in trouble, accused of being a rabble-rouser, and must defend himself before King Agrippa. It is commonly assumed that since Paul spent most of his ministry taking the gospel to the Greeks and Romans, he had abandoned the idea that the covenants were uniquely and exclusively for the Israelites. Yet, here, in Acts 26:6-7, near the very end of his life, Paul identifies the animating thrust of his entire ministry: *"And now I stand and am judged for the hope of the promise made of God unto our fathers: Unto which promise our twelve tribes, instantly serving God day and night, hope to come. For which hope's sake, king Agrippa, I am accused of the Jews."* It is clear that Paul anticipates the twelve tribes of Israel being central to God's plan. Why would he believe such a notion if ten of the tribes had been irreparably lost eight centuries earlier? Clearly that genetic stream must have

still existed, and Paul must have known where to find them if he harbored such a clear expectation.

Artist's impression of Saint Paul before Marcus Agrippa.

So, where were these tribes? The people of Rome comprised some of them. The Roman nation was genetic Israel whose forefathers had migrated to the Italian peninsula. God had divorced them from His covenant, but had not forgotten them. Now the time was ripe for their re-integration into the body of believers, and Paul was the man to spearhead this effort. He knew what he was doing and to whom he was speaking. Thus, we find clues laced into the text of the book of Romans. Let us consider some of them.

Remember now, the book of Romans was written to whom? The church at Rome, which was comprised of . . . Romans! Beginning in Romans 4:1, Paul wrote: *"What shall we say then that Abraham our father, as pertaining to the flesh, hath found?"* Notice he said to the Romans that Abraham was *"our father,"* not my father. Paul repeats this in Romans 4:12, referring to *"our father Abraham."* And in case one missed it, just a few verses later Paul says the following: *"Therefore it is of faith that it might be of grace; to the end the promise might be sure to all the seed; not to that only which is of the law, but to that also which is of the faith of Abraham, who*

is the father of us all, (as it is written, I have made thee a father of many nations) . . ." (Romans 4:16-17). Speaking to the Romans, Paul said that Abraham was the father of <u>us all</u>, not just those of the law (that is, the Jews or Judeans, of whom Paul was a part). Abraham was also father to others who no longer had the law, that is, nations like the Romans, and as we shall see, the Greeks.

Rembrant's depiction of Saint Paul in custody in Rome.

In Romans chapter 9, Paul begins a detailed discussion of God's elective choice in salvation. Imbedded in this discussion are more excellent clues. Consider Romans 9:4-5: *"Who are the Israelites; to whom pertaineth the adoption, and the glory, and the covenants, and the giving of the law, and the service of God, and the promises; Whose are the fathers, and of whom as concerning the flesh Christ came, who is over all, God blessed forever. Amen."* Please observe that Paul tells the Romans that all of these valued blessings are for Israelites–even the adoption, which many theologians assume is the vehicle by which non-Israelites would become part of God's plan. But consider this: why would any Israelite need to be adopted? It is only because they had been previously cut off from the covenant. Who was cut off? The ten tribes of Israel that were dispersed, only later to form into heathen nations in Europe, one of which was the Roman state. Thus, Paul is informing the Romans of the fact that God elected them out of Israel (Jacob) for future benefits. Romans 9:10 contains another simple clue showing that Paul knew who the Romans were: *"And not only this; but when Rebecca also had conceived by one, even by our father Isaac."* You see? Again, Paul stated to the Romans that Isaac was <u>our</u> father.

Romans 11 is an interesting section. Here Paul discussed the wild olive being grafted in, referring to the Romans as *"you Gentiles"* (verse 13). He said that *"thou, being a wild olive tree, wert graffed in among them,"* and should not boast (verses 17-18). What was Paul talking about? It is not difficult. The small Judean nation was the natural olive. The wild olive was divorced and dispersed Israel who had formed new nations in their eight-hundred-year hiatus from contact with Jehovah. These nations were called Gentiles. (remember that the word *Gentiles* simply means *nations*). The olive was a symbol of Israel in

Top: the Roman forum. Below: first century Christian art from the Roman catacombs, "The Good Shepherd."

the Old Testament. The context of this chapter is framed by Paul's prior comments when he said, *"Hath God cast away his people? God forbid"* (verse 1) and, *"God hath not cast away his people which he foreknew"* (verse 2). Who had been seemingly cast away? Divorced, dispersed, ten-tribed Northern Israel. What Paul was telling the Romans is simple: God has neither lost nor forgotten you! He went on and declared that *"blindness in part is happened to Israel, until the fulness of the Gentiles be come in"* (verse 25). What part of Israel was blinded? Many of the Judeans. Why? So the Gentiles, who were Israel in their divorced, pagan condition, could rejoin the covenant. Paul then immediately concluded with the statement, *"And so all Israel shall be saved"* (verse 26). How could all Israel be saved? Paul meant both parts, undivorced Judea (the natural olive) and the previously divorced ten-tribed Israel (the wild olive).

Let us continue the trek through the New Testament and move on to the Greeks. Paul wrote a number of epistles to Greek churches in Greek cities. Like the

Romans, and as already noted in a previous chapter, the Greeks were direct descendants of Israelites separated long before from their ancestral faith in Abraham, Isaac, and Jacob. While the majority of the Greeks had no knowledge of their roots, one can see from this passage in the Apocrypha that not all had been forgotten: *"This is a copy of the letter they sent to Onias: 'King Arius of the Spartans, to the high priest Onias, greetings. It has been found in writing concerning the Spartans and the Jews that they are brothers and are of the family of Abraham'"* (1 Maccabees 12:19). But let us look at the clues we derive from the writings of Paul as he writes to churches in various Greek cities of that time.

Renowned King
Leonidas of Sparta.

To the church in Corinth, one of the leading Greek cities and the host of the popular athletic Corinthian games, Paul stated this: *"Moreover, brethren, I would not that ye should be ignorant, how that all our fathers were under the cloud, and all passed through the sea; And were all baptized in the cloud and in the sea; And did all eat the same spiritual meat; and did all drink the same spiritual drink: for they drank of that spiritual Rock that followed them: and that Rock was Christ" (1 Corinthians 10:1-4).* Did you notice? Paul said *"all our fathers."* That is, the ancestors of the Corinthians were with Paul's ancestors in the wilderness after they left Egypt, crossed the Red Sea, were preserved by the cloudy pillar of God's presence, and received water from the rock that Moses struck. Paul was telling them that they are genetic Israelites.

Ruins of the ancient Greek city of Corinth.

To another group of people that lived in the Greek-speaking world Paul had a similar message. These were the Galatians. Although they spoke Greek by the first century A.D., the Gauls were actually of Celtic extraction. They were another group of Israelites in dispersion that had invaded Greek territory and settled in Asia Minor. Paul stated: *"Know ye therefore that they which are of faith are the children of Abraham" (Galatians 3:7).* Note that Paul did *not say* that people of faith are the *spiritual* children of Abraham, although that is what many theologians today incorrectly assume. He simply said they were the children of Abraham. What people of faith was Paul talking about? The church of the Galatians, that is, believers who were from Galatia. Paul was not stating or implying that such a notion as a spiritual Israelite existed. He was telling them that they were literal, genetic Israelites. If you need further proof of the identity of the Galatians, then go to Galatians 4:28-

29: *"Now we, brethren, as Isaac was, are the children of promise. But as then he that was born after the flesh persecuted him that was born after the Spirit, even so it is now."* This passage is often misinterpreted, but it need not be. Most assume that Isaac was the child of the flesh in that

he was a genetic descendant of his father Abraham, and that Paul was like Isaac in that he also was a genetic descendant of Abraham. Allegedly, the children of the Spirit are non-Israelites who are "adopted" or "grafted in." But that is all completely wrong. Look at Galatians chapter 4 more closely. This chapter contrasts the child of the flesh with the child of the Spirit/ promise. It contrasts Ishmael to Isaac. Which was which?

The Dying Gaul: this famed statue depicts an Israelitish Gaul who fought the Greeks in Asia Minor in the third century before Christ.

Of course, both were children of Abraham genetically, so what is really being discussed? The topic is the means by which each was brought into the world. Ishmael was the child of the flesh in that he was conceived through ordinary lustful means, involving the fears and passions of Abraham and Sarah. But Isaac was the child born through the miraculous work of God's Spirit, Who made pregnancy possible in an old woman. Isaac was the child of promise, born after the Spirit. Now look closely again at what Paul wrote to the Galatians in verse 28: *"Now we, brethren, as Isaac was, are the children of promise."* He is telling them that they are descendents of Abraham through Sarah. This is emphasized further in verse 31: *"So then, brethren, we are not children of the bondwoman, but of the free."* The bondwoman was Hagar. But the free woman was Sarah, and the Galatians were her descendants.

Leaving Paul, consider the plain and unmistakable words of James when he addressed his letter *"to the twelve tribes which are scattered abroad, greeting" (James 1:1)*. If the ten tribes had been lost forever, how and why would James have written an epistle to them? Obviously, he had some idea about who the descendants of the twelve tribes were.

Now turn your attention to Peter's writings. He wrote his first epistle to *"the strangers scattered throughout Pontus, Galatia, Cappadocia, Asia, and Bythynia" (1 Peter 1:1)*. These were all provinces of the land mass today called Turkey, or Asia Minor, but were then a core part of the Greek world. Now, who were these strangers? He lets us know more in chapter three in the midst of his exhortation to ladies regarding their duty to their husbands. Peter wrote this: *"For after this manner in the old time the holy women also, who trusted in God, adorned themselves, being in subjection to their own husbands: Even as Sara obeyed Abraham, calling him Lord: whose daughters ye are . . ." (1 Peter 3:5-6)*. Please observe that Peter has helped identify the strangers to whom he has written by narrowing their identity to the offspring of Sarah. These ladies are the daughters of Sarah and Abraham!

Renaisance painting
of Saint Peter preaching.

John received the great vision of Jesus Christ known as the book of Revelation. Does this book provide clues on our topic? Indeed it does. One cannot honestly read Revelation without discerning that Israel plays a uniquely central role. Three quick illustrations of this fact will be useful. First, the four remarkable beasts of Revelation 4:7 are in the image of the four ancient symbols of Israel: the lion, the calf, the man, and the eagle. Second, it is people from the tribes of Israel that are providentially sealed in chapter seven. Third, in chapter twenty-one, we see that the bride of Christ, which is the New Jerusalem, is built in such a manner that only the twelve tribes of Israel can enter into its precincts: *"And I John saw the holy city, new Jerusalem,*

coming down from God out of heaven, prepared as a bride adorned for her husband . . . And had a great wall and high, and had twelve gates, and at the gates twelve angels, and names written thereon, which are the names of the twelve tribes of the children of Israel"

Late Medieval painting of the New Jerusalem; notice the twelve gates.

(Revelation 21:2, 12). Do you see the significance? Only those who are of the twelve tribes can enter the New Jerusalem: the bride of Christ.

The people of Europe, many of them the direct descendants of the Romans and Greeks, have carried Christianity for two thousand years. Without Europe, Christianity would have died. Indeed, it would have never really been born. The people of Europe are genetic Israel, and Israel plays a uniquely central role in the New Testament.

As a final passage proving this point, consider Hebrews 8:7-10, which reads: *"For if that first covenant had been faultless, then should no place have been sought for the second. For finding fault with them, he saith, Behold the days come, saith the Lord, when I will make a new covenant with the house of Israel and with the house of Judah: Not according to the covenant that I made with their fathers in the day when I took them by the hand to lead them out of the land of Egypt, because they continued not in my covenant, and I regarded them not, saith the Lord. For this is the covenant that I will make with the house of Israel after those days, saith the Lord; I will put my laws into their minds, and write them in their hearts: and I will be to them a God, and they shall be to me a people."* The word "testament" simply means covenant. When we speak of the New Testament, we are speaking of the New Covenant. And according to St. Paul in the book of Hebrews, whom did God make the New Covenant with? Israel—only the twelve tribes of Israel comprised by its two houses, Judah and Israel. How does this prove that Europeans are descendants of Israel? Because with only the fewest of exceptions in two thousand years of Christian history, only the genetic offspring of Christian Europeans have borne New Testament fruit. It is the people descended from Christian Europe who have copied the Bible, translated the Bible, incorporated Bible law into their national framework, sent out masses of missionaries, built the great churches of the world, developed biblical theology, written the profound books of the faith, composed great biblical pieces of music, and created stunning works of biblical art. The people descended from Christian Europe alone have the fruit that proves they are Israel of old. After all, Jesus said, *"for the tree is known by his fruit"* (Matthew 12:33).

It is thus concluded that the writers of the New Testament knew that the people of Europe, including the Romans and the Greeks, were the literal, genetic offspring of ancient Israel. Paul, Peter, James, and John wrote with that thought in mind. It is clear that throughout the Christian era, these same people have had a uniquely high-profiled role in God's work in the earth. No longer do theologians need to strain to create a "spiritual Israel" that can be the inheritors of the New Covenant through "adoption" or "grafting in." The real, bona fide, genetic Israel has been active all along, doing the work of God and maintaining the culture of the Bible.

5

A Theological Perspective: Election and the Lost Sheep of the House of Israel

"Not all who wander are lost."
–J.R.R. Tolkien

Proving that people of Caucasian European extraction are the physical descendants of the ancient Israelites can be done in several ways. It is now the goal to provide reasonable evidence of this thesis from a theological perspective.

The beginning point of this discussion is the concept of election. Election is the idea that God, for reasons we may not always understand, chooses some person or group of people for some specific purpose. One type of election that Scripture teaches is election on an individual basis. For example, God chose the recipients of His salvation grace. In this case, the election is secret; no one knows who the elect in salvation are—not even the elect themselves. A second type of election taught in the Bible is collective, or the choosing of a group of people. This election is generally not secret, but is open information to everyone.

The Bible teaches both collective and individual election. A *broad* perspective reveals that God collectively elected the *entire people of Israel* for special purposes. From *within* that large mass, God also elected *some individual Israelites* to also receive His salvation grace. It is *broad collective election* that is the primary focus of this essay.

Collective Election in the Old Testament

Few Bible students attempt to disagree with the premise that God selected the Hebrew nation (Israelites) to be His chosen vessel of distinction in the Old Testament. Beginning with Abraham and narrowing the field to the descendants of one of Abraham's grandsons (Jacob), God chose them for His own purposes. This theme so permeates the Old Testament in its books of law and history that to deny it renders the narrative meaningless. A few passages illustrate this vital principle of election. To Abraham, God said, *"I will make of thee a great nation, and I will bless thee, and make thy name great; and thou shalt be a blessing: And I will bless them that bless thee, and curse him that curseth thee, and in thee shall all families of the earth be blessed" (Genesis 12:2-3).* At Mount Sinai, Jehovah had the following to say to the Israelite nation upon their reception of the Ten Commandments: *"Now therefore, if ye will obey my voice indeed, and keep my covenant, then ye shall be a peculiar treasure unto me above all people" (Exodus 19:5).*

Abraham, the chosen of God, sacrifices Isaac, by Gerhard van Reutern.

This covenant was exclusive, and was established under the leadership of one of the most remarkable men in history, Moses.

While the covenant at Mount Sinai was conditional, based on obedience, God made no such overtures to any other people. Indeed, God later promised that if they did break this covenant, He would chastise them for waywardness so that at least a remnant would be driven back to Him. Consider the extensive description of this in Leviticus 26. The entire passage is too lengthy to reprint here, but we can capture the flavor with these verses: *"But if ye will not hearken unto me, and will not do all these commandments; And if ye shall despise my statutes, or if your soul abhor my judgments, so that ye will not do all my commandments, but that ye break my covenant: I will also do this unto you . . . And I will set my face against you, and ye shall be slain before your enemies . . . And I will make your heaven as iron and your earth as brass . . . And I will also send wild beasts among*

Moses, by Michelangelo. The horns were added by the sculptor to mock an infamous blunder in the Latin Vulgate regarding its description of Moses.

you . . . And I will bring the land into desolation . . . And I will scatter you among the heathen . . . And ye shall perish among the heathen . . . And yet for all that, when they be in the land of their enemies, I will not cast them away, neither will I abhor them, to destroy them utterly, and to break my covenant with them: for I am the Lord their God. But I will for their sakes remember the covenant of their ancestors" (Leviticus 26:14,15, 17, 19, 22, 32, 33, 38, 44,45). Repeatedly, Moses chided the people to remember God, with mixed results. Yet God never forgot about Israel.

As we continue through the text of the Old Testament, the same tenor of God's everlasting love remains. Yes, the Israelites forgot God time and again, but then He punished them. This in turn stimulated a period of repentance in at least a portion of them, resulting in a renewal of their collective spiritual life. Thus we find scattered throughout the Old Testament passages such as Amos 3:2: *"You only have I known of all the families of the earth: therefore I will punish you for all your iniquities."* In fact, the last book of the Old Testament, Malachi, heightens this theme of punishing and purifying the people of Israel. Consider Malachi 3:3: *"And he shall sit as a refiner and purifier of silver: and he shall purify the sons of Levi, and purge them as gold and silver, that they may offer unto the Lord an offering in righteousness."* The final three verses of this prophet read as follows: *"Remember ye the law of Moses my servant, which I commanded unto him in Horeb* [Mt. Sinai] *for all Israel, with the statutes and judgments. Behold, I will send you Elijah the prophet before the coming of the great and dreadful day of the Lord: And he shall turn the heart of the fathers to the children, and the heart of the children to their fathers, lest I come and smite the earth with a curse"* (Malachi 4:3).

It is plain to see that the principle of God's unconditional election of Israel is a fixed cornerstone of the Old Testament. While the blessings of peace and prosperity may be withdrawn until they repent, Jehovah will never utterly and permanently abandon Israel.

Collective Election in the New Testament

Does this change in the New Testament? Bible students disagree. Some completely reject this concept of collective election and focus entirely on individual election and repentance. While individual election and repentance are highly profiled in the New Testament, it was present in the Old Testament all along.

Even in the days of the judges, kings, and prophets of ancient Israel, every man had to make his way to Jehovah in repentance if eternal life were to be his. The question before us is not regarding individual salvation in either the Old or New Testament, for in both cases every man must seek the face of God completely alone. The issue before us is this: does the New Testament abandon this theme of the collective election of Israel so highly profiled in the Old Testament?

The answer is an unqualified no. Israel is as highly profiled in the theology of the New Testament as the Old. Collectively speaking, Israel is to play a powerful and central role in all of God's work on earth until the end of time itself. Consider several very plain passages.

First, look at Paul's comments in Romans as he addressed this very point: *"I say then, Hath God cast away his people? God forbid. For I also am an Israelite, of the seed of Abraham, of the tribe of Benjamin. God hath not cast away his people which he foreknew . . ." (Romans 11:1-2).* Now consider what Paul said about Israel just two chapters previously: *"Who are Israelites; to whom pertaineth the adoption, and the glory, and the covenants, and the giving of the law, and the service of God, and the promises" (Romans 9:4).* It is quite clear that Paul embraced the idea of the collective election of Israel and did nothing to erode it.

Second, consider this passage in Hebrews, probably also written by Paul, which is crystal clear on Israel's continued special role in God's divine works: *" . . . Behold the days come, saith the Lord, when I will make a new covenant with the house of Israel and with the house of Judah . . .For this is the covenant that I will make with the house of Israel after those days, saith the Lord; I will put my laws into their mind, and write them in their hearts: and I will be to them a God, and they shall be to me a people" (Hebrews 8:8, 10).* Again, Israel is central to what God is doing on earth in the New Testament. In fact, notice that it clearly states that the New Covenant is with the same people as the Old Covenant was! There has been no change in God's choice of people.

A third passage should be sufficient to persuade any open-minded Bible student. Revelation describes the Bride of Christ, the New Jerusalem, at the final consummation of the ages, the climax of history. Of whom is this bride comprised? Only Israelites. See for yourself: *"And I John, saw the holy city, New Jerusalem, coming down from God out of heaven, prepared as a bride adorned for her husband . . .and he carried me away in the spirit to a great and high mountain, and showed me that great city, the holy Jerusalem, descending out of heaven from God . . . And had a great wall and high, and twelve gates, and on the gates twelve angels, and names written thereon, which are the names of the twelve tribes of Israel"* (Revelation 21:2,10,12).

Although more could be added easily, this evidence is decisive. Anyone who insists that Israel, in a collective sense, is not uniquely chosen of God in the New Testament, or in the New Covenant if you prefer that nomenclature, is either willingly ignorant, thoroughly duped, or dishonest.

Sheep: A Metaphor for Israel

Now that it has been ascertained that Israel was collectively chosen in the Old Testament and that unique selection has been maintained to this very moment, please consider a metaphor used for Israel in its collective sense. Many metaphorical images are used in the Bible, including lamps, olive trees, women, and candlesticks. But the most pervasively used metaphor for the Israelites is sheep. Indeed, some writers have simply called the Israelites the sheep people. Perhaps the image of a white, wooly, harmless, and slow-to-learn-from-his-mistakes sheep is descriptive of the national characteristics of Israelites. But even more important than any identifiable group characteristics of Israelites is the simple fact that the Bible repeatedly uses *sheep* as a descriptive term for these Hebrews. Here are just a few of many possible examples that could be cited:

Psalm 74:1-2 states, *"O God, why hast thou cast us off forever? Why dost thine anger smoke against the sheep of thy pasture? Remember thy congregation, which thou hast purchased of old; the rod of thine inheritance, which thou hast redeemed; this Mount Zion, wherein thou hast dwelt."*

Psalm 78:52-53 reads, *"But made his own people to go forth like sheep, and guided them in the wilderness like a flock. And he led them on safely, so that they feared not: but the sea overwhelmed their enemies."*

Psalm 79:13 says, *"So we thy people and sheep of thy pasture will give thee thanks for ever: we will shew forth thy praise to all generations."*

Psalm 100:3 declares: *"know ye that the Lord he is God: it is he that hath made us, and not we ourselves; we are his people, and the sheep of his pasture."*

Isaiah 40:9,11 reads, *"O Zion that bringest good tidings, get thee up into the high mountain: O Jerusalem that bringest good tidings, lift up thy voice with strength, lift it up, be not afraid; say unto the cities of Judah, Behold your God . . . He shall feed his flock like a shepherd: he shall gather the lambs with his arm, and carry them in his bosom, and shall gently lead those that are with young."*

Zechariah 9:16 says, *"And the Lord their God shall save them in that day as the flock of his people: for they shall* be as the stones of a crown, lifted up as an ensign upon his land."

Third century sculpture of Christ as the Good Shepherd.

In the Old Testament the metaphor of sheep or flocks refers only to Israel. For those that are skeptical, read the above verses in their larger context and you will see this is so. This imagery is never used to refer to another people or nation. Now, it is assumed that in the New Testament the metaphor of flocks and sheep is referring to a church body or a congregation—and it is. But many also assume that such a church body or congregation could be comprised of people that are not Israelites—but there is no proof of this anywhere in the New Testament. Indeed, it is only logical and fair to assume that the metaphor of sheep still refers only to Israel unless there is fresh use that is plainly otherwise—and there is none.

Other Sheep?

Remembering that God elects, chastens, and passes over groups and nations on a collective basis helps us understand an interesting passage in the New Testament about sheep. Consider Matthew 25:31-33: *"When the Son of man shall come in his glory, and all the holy angels with him, then shall he sit upon the throne of his glory: And before him shall be gathered all nations: and he shall separate them one from another, as a shepherd divideth his sheep from the goats: and he shall set the sheep on his right hand, but the goats on the left."* This judgment has many lessons for us, but the singular relevant point is the observation that this collective judgment of nations indicates that there is more than one sheep nation. There are multiple sheep nations and multiple goat nations that shall receive collective judgment.

But, if sheep can refer only to Israel, how can there be other sheep nations?

Quite simply really, if we remember the Old Testament prophecies regarding the Israelites. Israel was not to remain one nation, but was to become many nations. As God said to Jacob, *". . . thy name shall not be called any more Jacob, but Israel shall be thy name: and he called his name Israel, And God said unto him, I am God almighty: be fruitful and multiply; a nation and a company of nations shall be of thee, and kings shall come out of thy loins" (Genesis 35:10-11).* More specific prophecies of multiple nations coming from Israel are found in Genesis 48:19, Genesis 49:22-26, and Deuteronomy 33:17.

Byzantine mosaic of Christ separating the Sheep nations from the Goat nations.

So where are these other sheep nations?

In earlier chapters I have documented the historical data that conclusively shows that people of European Caucasian extraction are literal, genetic descendants of the ancient Israelites. Many other authors have written fine works making this historical linkage. Recapping, this evidence proves that the ten tribes of the Northern Kingdom of Israel, when taken into captivity by the Assyrians in 722 B.C., eventually escaped from their captors and, en masse, made a harrowing escape over the Caucasus Mountains. They migrated into western Europe over the next several hundred years, becoming the progenitors of the Anglo-Saxon, Nordic race. By the time of Jesus, these people were firmly entrenched in Western Europe.

However, the goal here is not to repeat this evidence, but show that there are scriptural clues that support this from the perspective of election. If these European nations were sheep nations, just like the Judean nation, why are there no references to them? Or are there?

Jospeh of Arimathea, also known as Joseph of Glastonbury, depicted in stained glass in Saint James Church in Picadilly, England.

Many will be surprised to discover that Jesus Himself knew about these Israelites who had been disconnected from the original branch for hundreds of years. When we reconstruct what is known about Jesus' personal life, it makes perfect sense that He knew. Let us recall that Jesus had already developed such an impressive base of knowledge at the age of twelve that He stunned the scholars at Jerusalem (Luke 2:41-52). Jesus became a man of great knowledge. Additionally, consider this connection: the man that gave up his own tomb after Jesus' death was His mother's uncle, Joseph of Arimathea, an international businessman with a cosmopolitan outlook. Joseph was wealthy and owned a shipping company that regularly plied the waters of the Mediterranean Sea. One of the products he commonly carried was tin, brought all the way from the "Tin Isles," or Britain. A persistent legend in Cornwall of southwest England is that Jesus accompanied His uncle on at least one of these journeys to obtain tin. Since the Bible records nothing of Jesus' life between the ages of twelve and thirty, it is quite plausible that He may in fact have actually visited Britain with His uncle during His youth, and the legends have a nugget of truth at their root.

Regarding scriptural proof, let us begin with John 7:35. When Jesus alluded in the preceding verses that He would soon be returning to heaven, the Pharisees misunderstood His meaning and said, *". . . Whither will he go, that we shall not find him? Will he go unto the dispersed among the gentiles, and teach the gentiles?"* Remembering that the word *gentiles* simply means *nations*, it is clear that the Pharisees knew that some Israelites of old had been separated from the Israelites that remained in Judea and were *somewhere out there* among other nations. Indeed, this verse proves that it was general knowledge among Judeans that other Isra-elites were out there some-where. Is it possible that Jesus knew this also?

A sheepfold

Absolutely, for He states as much, specifically referring to them as sheep, a word used to refer to Israelites: *"And other sheep I have, which are not of this fold: them also I must bring, and they shall hear my voice; and there shall be one fold, and one shepherd"* *(John 10:16)*. This statement quotes Ezekiel 37:24, a prophecy that the two ancient kingdoms of Israel (Israel and Judah) would be reunited under a Davidic king. When Jesus spoke these words, Ezekiel's prophecy was yet unfulfilled, as it is even today. You see, then, Jesus knew absolutely and positively that there were other Israelites *out there*, separate and distinct from the Israelites in Judea.

Another statement from Jesus' own lips provides final confirmation. The context for His comment comes when a non-Israelite woman who lived outside the confines of Judea (from the coasts of Tyre and Sidon) came to Jesus, seeking help for her daughter. Jesus eventually was moved by her determination and faith and helped her. But, before He did so, He explained to her that His main thrust outside of Judea was to Israelites, indeed lost Israelites: *"But he answered and said, I am not sent but unto the lost sheep of the house of Israel" (Matthew 15:24).* Note three things. First, sheep are again a metaphor for Israelites. Second, Jesus declares His target to be lost Israelites—not merely Israelites—but those who are lost. Third, the word *lost* cannot be interpreted to mean "individuals who are unsaved," because this passage is speaking collectively, not individually. We know Jesus was speaking collectively by the words, *"house of Israel."* Such a phrase is a collective term, a group term, a national characterization. Thus, the true meaning of Jesus' response is something like, "Madam, you do not live in the land of Judea, and the only folks outside of Judea I am really meant to target are dispersed Israelites who have become completely disconnected from their covenant past."

It thus becomes quite clear that the *"lost sheep of the house of Israel,"* the *"other sheep which are not of this fold,"* and the *"dispersed among the gentiles"* are Israelites that were previously severed from the body of Israelites still living in the land of Judea in the days of Jesus. These people were still part of God's divine plan of collective election. Can they be identified?

Identifying the Other Sheep:
The Lost Sheep of the House of Israel

The lost sheep of the House of Israel, these other sheep that were dispersed among the Gentiles, can be identified because they, as a group, heard the voice of their shepherd and responded. Hearing and responding in a positive way is the hallmark we are looking for in this mysterious group. You see, the New Testament teaches that Jesus' people, these sheep people, are the ones who would hear His voice, listen to the Gospel of Jesus Christ when spread by His apostles, and actually believe it, act upon it, and begin reshaping their society to be Christian.

Have a look at the passages in Scripture that tell us that Jesus' people will hear Him and respond favorably:

John 10:3-4 reads, *"To him the porter openeth; and the sheep hear his voice: and he calleth his own sheep by name, and leadeth them out. And when he putteth forth his own sheep, he goeth before them, and the sheep follow him: for they know his voice."*

John 10:26-27 states, *"But ye believe not, because ye are not of my sheep, as I said unto you. My sheep hear my voice, and I know them, and they follow me."*

1 John 2:19 asserts, *"They went out from us, but they were not of us; for if they had been of us, they would have no doubt continued with us: but they went out, that they might be made manifest they were not all of us."*

John 8:39 declares, *". . . If ye were Abraham's children, ye would do the works of Abraham."*

Matthew 12:33 reads, *"Either make the tree good, and his fruit good; or else make the tree corrupt, and his fruit corrupt: for the tree is known by his fruit."*

Matthew 7:16-17, 20 says, *"Ye shall know them by their fruits. Do men gather grapes of thorns, or figs of thistles? Even so every good tree bringeth forth good fruit: but a corrupt tree bringeth forth evil fruit . . . Wherefore by their fruits ye shall know them."*

Now then, speaking collectively about nations—not individuals, but speaking in terms of God's election of nations to accomplish His purposes in the earth, what nations over the past two thousand years have done the work of God? Is there any nation, cluster of nations, peoples, races, or ethnicities that have embraced the teachings of Christ above other nations and peoples? Where can we find the sheep nations of Matthew 25:32? What nations have heard the voice of Jesus, their shepherd, and followed Him? What nations have done the works of Abraham? What nations have exhibited the good fruit of the gospel of Christ? From what nations have the missionaries come? Where did the great evangelists receive their training to go forth with the gospel of Christ?

Saint Etienne Cathedral
in Bourges, France

Again, this is looking at world history for the past two thousand years and examining the Christian fruit of nations. Yes, within nations are found good and evil men, Christians and unbelievers; but that atomized individual examination is not what is being spoken of here. The question is this: what nation or nations have collectively been doing the work of Christ for the past two thousand years?

Are there any nations that stand out from the others on planet earth that have built great churches to the exultation of Christ? Where are the nations that have established colleges and schools to teach the Word of God and to spread the Gospel of Christ? Where can we find nations that have framed the Ten Commandments of God as cornerstones of their law codes? What nations have created Christian institutions that incorporate the teachings of Jesus into their social order? Are there any nations that have created a Christian society?

What nations feed other people when starvation and famine strike? Are there any nations that respond with compassion to earthquake and flood victims in far away places? Where can we find the nations that bless others with their generosity in foreign aid to help the sick, diseased, poverty-ridden peoples of our planet? What nations send their sons to keep the peace in far away places wracked and riven in civil war? What nations send their fleets to police the sea-lanes, keeping them free and safe so the all people of the world can enjoy commerce and trade?

Where are these Christian nations that have been filled with good Christian works and have been a blessing to everyone on planet earth?

The answer by now should be clear: these nations are the Caucasian countries of European extraction. Only this group of nations bears the mark of God's work over the past two thousand years. Thus, returning

US Navy helicopter distributes aid to Asian tsunami victims.

to the original point, it is manifestly plain that the nations of the West—Britain, France, Germany, Scandinavia, the United States, and related Caucasian nations—are the Hebrews of old because they have borne the fruit of Christendom over many centuries. Certainly not every Caucasian/Israelite person within these lands has been elected to salvation, but that does not preclude the broad evidence that these nations are the "sheep nations" of the Bible and have collectively been elected to accomplish great things for God on the earth. It is they who are the *"lost sheep of the house of Israel" (Matthew 15:24).*

6

The Davidic Covenant and British Royal Genealogy

"When beggars die there
are no comets seen; but the heavens
themselves blaze forth the death of princes."
—William Shakespeare, *Julius Caesar*

Yet another method to show that Europeans are direct descendants of the ancient Hebrews is through the covenantal genealogy of royal houses of Europe, and more particularly, the British. It is common knowledge that many of the royal houses of Europe are closely related, but of all of them, the British throne has the most direct connection to the royalty of ancient Israel, the house of David.

God made an unconditional covenant with David that he would always have a natural descendant that would reign over Israel. *"But my mercy shall not depart away from him, as I took it from Saul, whom I put away before thee. And thine house and thy kingdom shall be established for ever before thee: the throne shall be established for ever"* *(2 Sam. 7:15-16).* It was this promise that Jehovah made with David by the mouth of Nathan the prophet which is still as binding today as it was when uttered 3,000 years ago. One of several perpetual covenants that God made, it is verified in numerous locations throughout the Bible (see 2 Samuel 23:5, 1 Kings 9:5, 1 Chronicles

28:4-7, Psalm 89:4,29-27, and Jeremiah 33:17-21,25-26). But it actually preceded David's own lifetime and continues to be in effect today. Truly, this covenant is a thread of truth woven into the biblical tapestry from Genesis to Revelation and is central to the scriptural theme of God's love for His people, Israel.

The Origins of the Davidic Covenant

One of the most remarkable aspects of this narrative is the physical symbol that God has used to bear witness to the continuity of His promise. In Genesis 28:11-22 Jacob dreamed of a ladder ascending to heaven. He awoke and used the stone he had

Jacob's ladder and the stony pillow that was to have a remarkable history.

claimed as a pillow to act as the physical symbol of his vow that he had contracted with Jehovah. This pillar was set in a place he called Bethel. In Genesis 35:11 Jacob receives this promise: *"And God said unto him, I am the God Almighty: be fruitful and multiply: a nation shall be of thee, and the kings shall come out of thy loins."* In verses 14 and 15 we find that Jacob commemorated this with an anointing upon a pillar in Bethel, no doubt the same one that had been his pillow: *"And Jacob set up a pillar in the place where he talked with him, even a pillar of stone: and he poured a drink offering thereon, and he poured oil thereon. And Jacob called the name of the place where God spake with him, Bethel."* This pillar or stone is significant because it typifies Jesus Christ as being the anointed one in whose veins flowed the royal blood of Jacob and David. Furthermore, it was customary for the Davidic kings to be coronated on a stone or pillar, this very same rock (2 Kings 11: 13-14). This became a tradition that was to have an extraordinary history of its own.

We find another event with great implications in Genesis 38: 24-30 concerning the birthing of twin sons to Judah, Pharez and Zarah. Note verses 28-30: *"And it came to pass, when she travailed, that the one put out his hand: and the midwife took and bound upon his hand a scarlet thread, saying, This came out first. And it came to pass, as he drew back his hand, that, behold, his brother came out: and she said, How hast thou broken forth? This breach came upon thee: therefore his name was called Pharez. And afterward came out his brother, that had the scarlet thread upon his hand: and his name was called Zarah."* This "breach" that was to be upon Pharaz was to have far reaching prophetic significance, as was also Zarah's scarlet thread. It is critical to remember that Jacob's deathbed prophecy regarding Judah was that he would be the royal tribe, and his seed was to be secure until the second coming of Jesus Christ: *"The sceptre shall not depart from Judah, nor a lawgiver from between his feet, until Shiloh come; and unto him shall the gathering of the people be"* (Genesis 49:10).

A third clue that may assist us in our search is found in the prophecy given to Joseph in Genesis 49: 24: *" But his bow abode in strength, and the arms of his hands were made strong by the hands of the mighty God of Jacob; (from thence is the shepherd, the stone of Israel)"*. In this parenthetical statement, the word "thence" indicates that the stone, Jacob's pillar, which was to become the coronation stone of the Davidic kings, would come from the geographical territory of Joseph. This can, in fact, be verified because Bethel was part of Joseph's tribal inheritance, and Bethel was where Jacob set up his pillar originally. Based on this passage, it can be plausibly argued that if we can identify where the tribe of Joseph can be found today, we should be able to locate the throne. On that throne will be a monarch of the tribe of Judah, yet ruling over a territory of Joseph.

The Davidic Family Tree
Is Nearly Destroyed

To track this story through the annals of history, let us pick up the story in the Old Testament. After the death of Solomon and the subsequent splitting of the kingdom, the Davidic kings of the southern kingdom of Judah continued to reign. Many people had a false sense of national invulnerability because of this convenant with David. How could their kingdom end if God promised there would always be a descendant of David ruling? Little did they realize that the "breach" of Genesis 38:29 was about to be fulfilled. How great must have been their shock when Jerusalem was captured and the apparent end of the Davidic line of kings came in 586 B.C.! Nebuchadanezzar and his Babylonian army took the city and captured Zedekiah as he fled with all his sons. Zedekiah, the last king, saw his sons slain before his very eyes. Then, blinded, with these stinging final images in his memory, he was exiled to die in Babylon (Jer.39:4-8).

Zedekiah's sons slain by Nebuchadnezzar, by Dore'

But this was not the end! According to biblical law, when there was no male heir the inheritance could be passed through a female if she married within her tribe (Num. 27:8, 36:6-8). Unknown to Nebuchadnezzar, Zedekiah's daughters survived and were thus legitimately able to inherit the throne. Escorted by a substantial contingent of fleeing Judeans, they were taken to the Egyptian border town of Tahpanhes, just out of the reach of Nebuchadnezzar. Jeremiah warned this multitude not to flee to Egypt to try avoiding the judgment of God; they would be better off remaining and taking their hard knocks. This advice was rejected, and most of them did not get the relief they sought. Ironically, however, a handful escaped from Egypt, including the all important daughters of Zedekiah. *"None shall return but such as shall escape" (Jer. 44:14).* Thus, in God's sovereignty, the disobedience of this fleeing contingent was the very vehicle He used to preserve David's lineage, for Zedekiah's daughters were among the tiny remnant to escape Egypt's collapse: *"And the remnant that is escaped of the house of Judah shall take root downward, and bear fruit upward: For out of Jerusalem shall go forth a remnant, and they that escape out of the mount Zion: the zeal of the LORD of hosts shall do this" (Is. 37:31-32).*

Riddles from Ezekiel the Prophet

As a prophet, Ezekiel stands as one of the most highly profiled. The son of a priest, he was taken to Babylon in the captivity of Jehoiachin, eleven years before the destruction of Jerusalem. He was settled in a community of Hebrew exiles by the banks of a large "river" or canal, known as Chebar. The mission of Ezekiel was one of comfort to the many captives in the land of Babylon. The major thread of his prophecies was that God was justified in permitting the captivity of His people. In fact, this was a sign of God's enduring love for His people in that they were suffering chastisement rather than being completely destroyed, as had been the case with other nations that had committed similar abominations. The seventeenth chapter of Ezekiel offers a great panorama of the various historical forces that were at play during this time and their relationship to Bible prophecy. It takes the form of riddles, not for the purpose of hiding the meaning, but to make the lesson more memorable: *"And the word of the the LORD came unto me, saying, Son of man, put forth a riddle, and speak a parable unto the house of Israel; And say, Thus saith the Lord GOD; A great eagle with great wings, longwinged, full of feathers, which had divers colours, came unto Lebanon, and took the highest branch of the cedar: He cropped off the top of his young twigs, and carried if into a land of traffick; he set it in a city of merchants. He took a fruitful tree. And it grew, and became a spreading vine of low stature, whose branches turned toward him, and the roots thereof were under him: so it became a vine, and brought forth branches, and shot forth sprigs"* (Ezekiel 17:1-6).

This first riddle is explained somewhat in verses 12-14 of this same chapter. From these verses and from what is known from historical context, the message becomes clear. The *"great eagle"* is Nebuchadnezzar and the Babylonian Empire. He is the king of birds and lives on spoil. His dominions spread far and wide, like *"great wings."* This eagle is *"full of feathers,"* indicating the many nations and peoples that comprised his empire. The *"divers colors"* represents the diversity of nations in his empire and the splendid nature of his court. Nebuchadnezzar had carried off Jehoiachin (also called Jeconiah) and many of his mighty men into captivity in Babylon when the latter was only eighteen years of age and had reigned but three months. In this parable, Jerusalem is likened to *"Lebanon,"* that is a *"forest"* of houses. The *"cedar"* is the royal family, and the *"highest branch"* is the young king Jehoiachin. Babylon is the *"land of traffick"* and the *"city of merchants"* where it was set. When Joiachin was carried away, Nebuchadnezzar took his uncle Mattaniah and placed him upon the throne in Jerusalem as a puppet ruler and changed his name to Zedekiah. As a native-born Judean, Zedekiah was of the *"seed of the land planted in a fruitful field."* This new Judean kingdom was figuratively by *"great waters"* in that it was now a vassal state of Babylon. As a *"willow tree,"* it was expected to grow rapidly as it drew political and economic strength from the empire, but was not expected to become a tall, stately tree that could be a competitor to Babylon; rather, *"a spreading vine of low stature."* It is important to note that Zedekiah *"made a covenant with him, and hath taken an oath of him" (Ezekiel 17:13);* that is, he was forced to take an oath of allegiance. Ezekiel 17:14 is significant concerning God's plan of chastisement for the Kingdom of Judah: *"That the kingdom might be base, that it might not lift itself up, but that by keeping of his covenant it might stand."* While the kingdom would be relatively weak, it would still remain! This was God's way of humbling the nation and encouraging them to turn to Him in repentance.

Cedar of Lebanon

How sad it is that they failed to see the hand of God in these events! Had Zedekiah been true to his oath and loyal to the king of Babylon, as he was at the first, his kingdom would have continued to grow and prosper (see verse 6). If he had led his people in repentance, an opportunity to regain the former dignity would have appeared that did not require a violation of his oath of loyalty.

Now the second riddle reveals the true nature of Zedekiah: *"There was also another great eagle with great wings and many feathers: and, behold, this vine did bend her roots toward him, and shot forth her branches toward him, that he might water it by the furrows of her plantation. It was planted in a good soil by great waters, that it might bring forth branches, and that it might bear fruit, that it might be a goodly vine" (Ezekiel 17:7-8).*

This second *"great eagle"* is the king of Egypt, the only other world power aside from Babylon. It also had *"great wings"* or a vast domain, and *"many feathers,"* or peoples. Zedekiah, represented as the vine, *"bent his roots"* toward this eagle, meaning he made secret overtures to the king of Egypt. Later, he *"shot forth his branches"* toward Egypt, indicating the above-board seeking of an alliance. The purpose of this alliance was to gain aid against Babylon or be *"watered by the furrows of her plantation."* The rebellion of Zedekiah is unequivocally condemned by God, despite the fact that he was in rebellion against an ungodly pagan king: *"As I live, saith the Lord God, surely in the place where the king dwelleth that made him king, whose oath he despised, and whose covenant he brake, even with him in the midst of Babylon he shall die" (Ezekiel 17:16).* The reality was he had sworn an oath of loyalty by the name of God, and the breaking of such an oath was repugnant and blasphemous to God. An oath to a king demands a sober outlook: *"I counsel thee to keep the king's commandment, and that in regard of the oath of God" (Ecclesiastes 8:2).* Rebellion is the opposite response of repentance. God sought repentance on the part of Zedekiah and the people toward Him. Instead, rebellion was fomented against the rod of divine chastisement. For this Zedekiah was condemned to die in the land of Babylon. The alliance he had sought with Egypt proved to be faulty. The Babylonian army had besieged Jerusalem, and although they lifted the siege when the Egyptian army approached, they returned as soon as the Egyptian army was forced out of the field of combat. As we have already seen, the city of Jerusalem was taken, and a desperate midnight escape attempt by Zedekiah proved futile. He was taken before Nebuchadnezzar, saw his sons slain before him, had his eyes put out, and was taken in shackles to Babylon to live out his days in obscurity (Ezekiel 17:16-21, Jeremiah 52:4-11).

The rebellion of Zedekiah brought the royal house of David to an inglorious end, or so it seemed. But the unbelief of man does not invalidate the promise of God! What was the promise of God? *"But my mercy shall depart away from him, as I took it from Saul, whom I put away before thee. And thine house and thy kingdom shall be established for ever before thee: thy throne shall be established for ever"* (II Samuel 7:15-16). *"Once have I sworn by my holiness that I will not lie unto David. His seed shall endure forever, and his throne as the sun before me. It shall be established for ever as the moon, and as a faithful witness in heaven. Selah"* (Psalm 89:35-37).

Jehovah's covenant with David is clear and unmistakable (see also Genesis 49:10, I Chronicles 28:4-7, Jeremiah 33:17-26). Those who spiritualize the throne of David by placing it only in the heart of the believer or in some heavenly celestial realm cheapen the power and reality of God's Word. Where, then, can it be found? Before that question can be answered, the third riddle of Ezekiel 17 will demonstrate the reality of this promise: *"Thus saith the Lord God; I will also take of the highest branch of the high cedar, and will set it; I will crop off from the top of his young twigs a tender one, and will plant it up on an high mountain and eminent: In the mountain of the height of Israel will I plant it: and it shall bring forth boughs, and bear fruit, and be a goodly cedar: and under it shall dwell all fowl of every wing; in the shadow of the branches thereof shall they dwell. And all the trees of the field shall know that I the LORD have brought down the high tree, have exalted the low tree, have dried up the green tree, and have made the dry tree to flourish: I the LORD have spoken and have done it"* (Ezekiel 17:22-24).

The meaning of this third riddle contains the vehicle by which God was to maintain the continuity of His promise. The *"high cedar"* is the House of David; the *"highest branch"* is King Zedekiah and his royal family; the *"young twigs"* are his children; *"a tender one"* represents a female member of this royal family;

and the *"high mountain"* represents a nation rising on the stage of world history. The meaning is that God would cause a daughter of King Zedekiah to be taken from Jerusalem and *"planted"* or married into another royal family in an Israelite nation. From this union would come *"boughs"* and *"fruit,"* meaning offspring, and from this fruit will come a *"goodly cedar"* or royal dynasty. The *"high tree"* and *"green tree"* that are brought down and dried up represent the Pharez line of the tribe of Judah from which David and Zedekiah were descended. The *"low tree"* and *"dry tree"* are symbolic of the Zarah line of Judah, which also was a dynasty of kings, but was in dispersion and had never entered the Land of Promise. The family into which Zedekiah's daughter married was of the lineage of Zarah; thus, after the Pharez dynasty no longer reigned over any Hebrews, the Zarah dynasty continued to reign and became preeminent.

So whom did this daughter of Zedekiah marry? Where did she go, and how did she get there? To what does *"overturn"* refer? The Bible narrative ends here, but other historical resources fill in. To these we must turn.

Lia Fail, the Stone of Destiny

From the histories of Dioderus, Hecataeus, Irish poets, and Scottish sources, the destiny of Zarah and of Zedekiah's daughter can be reconstructed. Zarah's family left Palestine while the tribes were yet in Egypt (about 1600 B.C.). Having failed to gain the sceptre in Judah, they left a trail of cities and dynasties behind in Asia Minor, the Mediterranean, and Europe. These include Troy, founded by Darda (1Chron.2:6), and New Troy (founded 1103 B.C.), later called Londinium by the Romans. Eventually as we descend the family tree, we are taken to Ireland where Eochaidh reigned as Ard-Righ (High King) concurrent with Jerusalem's destruction by the Babylonians.

It was at this time, the sixth century B.C., that a royal party of Judeans arrived from Egypt via Spain. Jeremiah (known as

Ollam Fodhla), Baruch the scribe, and Tea Tephi (daughter of the last king of Judah), were three notables among this small group. They brought with them of number of relics, including a large stone which subsequently was used as the royal inaugural stone at Tara and became known as Lia Fail, the Stone of Destiny. (The monolith presently at the site of Tara's Hill today is not the original.) Eochaidh and Tea Tephi were married and established

a new dynasty joining the Pharez and Zarah lines together. This new dynasty in the new land of Ireland represents the first *"overturn"* of Ezekiel 21:27. It also fulfilled the life mission of Jeremiah. *"See, I have this day set thee over the nations and over the kingdoms, to root out, and to pull down, and to destroy, and to throw down, to build, and to plant"* *(Jeremiah 1:10).*

An aerial view of Tara's Hill in County Meath, Ireland.

It is interesting to note that even to this, one of the more pre-eminent heraldic symbols used in Northern Ireland is the Red Hand of Ulster with a red cord around the wrist. This is certainly a link to Zarah's scarlet thread.

Moving forward in time, the second *"overturn"* occurred about 500 A.D. when Fergus More, brother of the King of Ireland, Muircheartach, invaded the western coast of Scotland. He established himself king in this new location over some conquered Picts and a large contingent of Irish immigrants who accompanied him. Desiring to be coronated upon Lia Fail (Stone of Destiny), he asked his brother to send it to Scotland for this purpose. Muircheartach granted his request, and there the stone remained for sometime. This event represents the second *"overturn."* It was first placed in Dunadd, a large hilltop fort, used by Fergus as his capital. Later it was to Iona, then to Dunstaffage; but wherever it went, it was the official coronation stone upon which the Davidic Kings of Scotland were crowned.

Finally, in 843 A.D., Kenneth MacAlphin moved Lia Fail to Scone, commemorating a victory that finally brought the remaining Picts under Scottish dominion. There it rested for over four centuries, thereby gaining the name "Stone of Scone."

Leaping forward again through time, we discover that the last years of the thirteenth century saw a number of claimants vying for the Scottish throne. In order to settle the dispute, Edward I of England was asked to arbitrate in order to prevent the civil war. He did so, but demanded that the Scots recognize his nominal suzerainty over Scotland (Actually, he was also a Davidic king and descendant of Kenneth Macalpin.). In 1296, Edward removed the Stone of

The coronation chair with the Stone of Scone. This chair was commisioned by Edward I when he took the stone from Scotland to London in 1296. This throne chair remains in Westminster Abbey.

Scone and placed it in Westminster Abbey. It was held in very high esteem by Edward, and he had a tall chair built to hold the stone. This became known as "Saint Edward's Chair" and has been used for the coronation of every English monarch since (except Mary Tudor, known as "Bloody Mary"). This was the third and final *"overturn,"* representing a change from one Davidic dynasty to another.

The physical return of the stone to Scotland in 1996 does not represent another "overturn" because it will be returned to London for future coronations. Furthermore, no change in dynasty or political structure accompanied its 1996 geographical change.

The stone itself bears witness to its remarkable past. Its dimensions are roughly rectangular, approximately 26" x 16" x 10". Two rust resistant iron alloy rings are imbedded in its surface, one at each end, apparently for carrying purposes. A deep groove runs between the rings, prob-

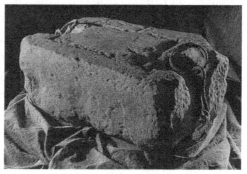

Lia Fail, the Stone of Destiny, or the Stone of Scone. It presently rests in Edinburgh Castle, Scotland.

ably worn from being carried around on a stout pole. It is composed of calcareous sandstone, not native to England—in fact, there are no known rock formations that match the stone in the British Isles. There is, however, a strata of sandstone that has been identified by a noted geologist as identical to the Stone of Scone near Bethel in Palestine!

Until the Return of King Jesus

The throne and stone have both come to rest until the end of the age. The British Isles and the Anglo-Saxon race that dwells there are the living elements of the tribe of Ephraim. The throne is occupied by a member of the House of David, descended from the tribe of Judah, residing in the land of Joseph, the birthright tribe. But the throne does not belong to any descendant of David;

they are mere keepers for the true owner, none other than our Savior Jesus Christ: *"He shall be great, and shall be called the Son of the Highest: and the LORD God shall give unto him the throne of his father David: And he shall reign over the house of Jacob for ever: and of his kingdom there shall be no end"* (*Luke 1:32-33*). Jesus Christ's first coming was as a Prophet. His ascension into heaven was in fulfillment of His role as Priest. But His return to earth will be as a King! We may not know the day or the hour, but His return may be imminent. He shall claim the throne that is rightfully His! *"And the seventh angel sounded; and there were great voices in heaven, saying, The kingdoms of this world are become the kingdoms of our LORD, and of Christ; and he shall reign forever and ever"* (*Revelation 11:15*).

The Genealogical Table

For those who are interested, what follows is a list of names of descendants of Abraham. It forks at Judah, the son of Jacob, and his twin sons Pharez and Zarah, both born from the lady Tamar. This list shows the direct descent, without interruption, of these two branches of Judah. It takes the reader through King David, down to the last King of Judah, Zedekiah. The list shows how the two branches were reunified in the marriage of Tea Tephi to Eochaidh, the High King of Ireland. Then the descent is shown, without interruption, through kings of Ireland and Scotland to the present royal house of Britain and the current reigning monarch, Queen Elizabeth II.

Following the ancient principle of primogenitor, most of the names are male. However, there are occasions of descent through the female and these are noted with an asterisk (*). It is worth noting that this table is highly simplified. There are multiple genetic paths by which Queen Elizabeth II is a direct descendant of King David of ancient Israel. To show all of the ways would be too complex for display here. The lineage selected is one of the most direct pathways. The most useful source for this research was Dennis M. Whitney of Royal House Publishing, PO Box 2525, Van Nuys, California 91404.

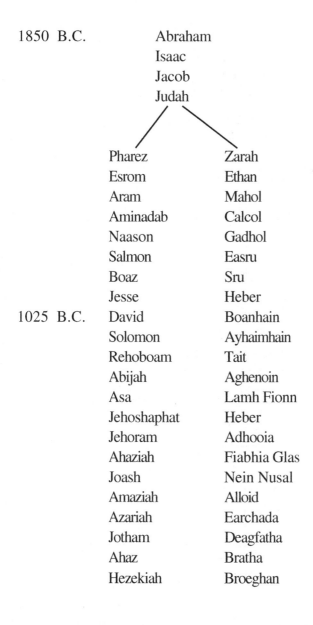

1850 B.C.   Abraham
Isaac
Jacob
Judah

Pharez	Zarah
Esrom	Ethan
Aram	Mahol
Aminadab	Calcol
Naason	Gadhol
Salmon	Easru
Boaz	Sru
Jesse	Heber
1025 B.C. David	Boanhain
Solomon	Ayhaimhain
Rehoboam	Tait
Abijah	Aghenoin
Asa	Lamh Fionn
Jehoshaphat	Heber
Jehoram	Adhooia
Ahaziah	Fiabhia Glas
Joash	Nein Nusal
Amaziah	Alloid
Azariah	Earchada
Jotham	Deagfatha
Ahaz	Bratha
Hezekiah	Broeghan

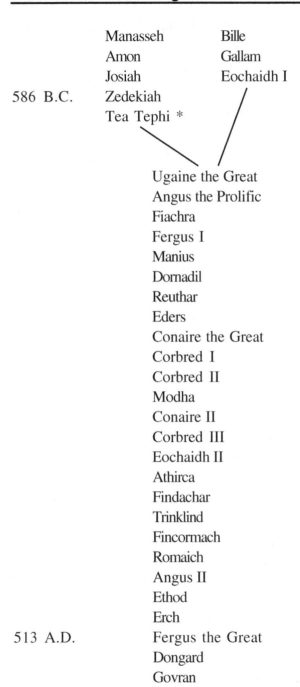

Manasseh   Bille
Amon   Gallam
Josiah   Eochaidh I

586 B.C.   Zedekiah
Tea Tephi *

Ugaine the Great
Angus the Prolific
Fiachra
Fergus I
Manius
Dornadil
Reuthar
Eders
Conaire the Great
Corbred I
Corbred II
Modha
Conaire II
Corbred III
Eochaidh II
Athirca
Findachar
Trinklind
Fincormach
Romaich
Angus II
Ethod
Erch

513 A.D.   Fergus the Great
Dongard
Govran

Aydan
Eugene
Donald
Ethach
Ethdre
Ethafind
Ethas
Alpin
839 A.D.   Kenneth McAlpin
Constantine II
Donald VI
Malcolm I
Kenneth II
Malcolm II
Beatrix *
Duncan I
David
Henry
Daviid
Isobel*
Robert the Competitor
Robert
1306 A.D.   Robert the Bruce
Marjory*
Robert II
Robert III
James I
James II
James III
James IV
James V
1587 A.D.   Mary Queen of Scots *
James VI of Scotland, I of England

	Elizabeth Stuart *
	Sophia *
	George I
	George II
	Frederick, Prince of Wales
1776 A.D.	George III
	Edward, Duke of Kent
	Victoria *
	Edward VII
	George V
	George VI
2013 A.D.	Elizabeth II
	Charles, Prince of Wales
	William, Duke of Cambridge

7

The Levitical Covenant and British History

*"And ye shall be unto me a
kingdom of priests, and an holy nation."*
–Exodus 19:6

Among the sundry important covenants found in Scripture, one of the least emphasized is the Levitical Covenant. The essence of this covenant is that God promised that there would always exist a cadre of men who would serve Jehovah and true biblical Israelites in the office of the priest. That is, no period of history would be completely bereft of spiritual leadership. But the covenant goes further than that, for not only would this spiritual leadership be filled at all times, but the promise of God was that there would be a genetic continuity from ancient times to the present. Thus, literal genetic descendants of ancient Levi must be alive today, somewhere on this planet. If we can find these Levites, these ministers of God, then we may be able to find the "lost ten tribes of Israel."

This does not mean that such men, if they could be identified, would exercise their responsibility in full knowledge, power, and virtue of biblical truth. Indeed, there were priests of varying qualities in ancient Israel, and some left much to be desired.

Nonetheless, God made clear promises that He would maintain the Levitic priesthood in the earth. Before we consider these promises, let it be stated that the continued existence of such a priesthood does not impinge on the majestic priesthood of Jesus Christ, Who overshadows all human spiritual offices by an infinite degree. Jesus Christ is of the Order of Melchizedek and is the only person to fill that exalted position. As it states in Hebrews 7:3, this order is *"without father, without mother, without descent, having neither beginning of days, nor end of life; but made like unto the Son of God; abideth a priest continually."* Jesus Christ, officiating as the Priest of the Order of Melchizedek and subjecting Himself as the perfect lamb without blemish, superceded all ordinary bloody sacrifices, and by His own blood made the Law of Blood Sacrifice permanently effective, thus making further bloody sacrifices by a human priesthood unnecessary. But that does not mean the Levitical priesthood was abolished. Neither was the need for Christ's sacrifice to be appropriated to the people in true repentance abrogated.

Eternal Biblical Promises

The Bible makes it plain that the Levitic Covenant must still be in force today! Consider the following passages. Genesis 49:10 states: *"The sceptre shall not depart from Judah, nor a lawgiver from between his feet, until Shiloh come; and unto him shall the gathering of the people be."* The lawgiver is the priesthood. The coming of Shiloh refers to the Second Coming of Jesus Christ, an event plainly yet in the future. Therefore the priesthood should be found in the earth today. Where? This verse provides an important clue when it states that the lawgiver will be found between the feet of the sceptre of Judah, the royal Davidic throne. Find the Davidic throne on planet earth today, and the priesthood will be nearby.

A clearer passage that speaks of the enduring Levitic Covenant is found in Jeremiah 33:17-21. It also ties the throne of David together with the Levitical Covenant. *"For thus saith the LORD; David shall never want a man to sit upon the throne of the house of Israel; Neither shall the priests the Levites want a man before me to offer burnt offerings, and to kindle meat offerings, and to do sacrifice continually. And the word of the Lord came unto Jeremiah, saying, Thus saith the Lord, If ye can break my covenant of the day, and my covenant of the night, and that there should not be day and night in their season; Then may also my covenant be*

A depiction of the consecration of Aaron in Exodus 28:1.

broken with David my servant, that he should not have a son to reign upon his throne; and with the Levites the priests my ministers." Do day and night maintain their rhythm? Of course they do. It is thus plain for all to see that <u>somewhere</u> there are genetic Levites, that is, true ministers of God, keeping faith with Him.

Other passages add considerable weight to this concept. In Numbers 25:13 we discover that one of the direct descendants of Levi was rewarded for his zeal with a covenant of his own. This was Phinehas, the grandson of Aaron of whom God said, *"And he shall have it, and his seed after him, even the covenant of an everlasting priesthood . . . ."* So, somewhere on this orb we call earth, the offspring of Phinehas are acting as faithful men of God.

In Jeremiah 35 we are introduced to the clan of the Rechabites, a branch of the Levitical tree who are blessed uniquely for their devotion to the instructions of their forefather Jonadab, the son Rechab. Of them Jeremiah 35:19 states, *"Therefore, thus saith the Lord of hosts, the God of Israel, Jonadab, the son of Rechab shall not want a man to stand before me for ever."* Again, if the Bible be true, there must be living flesh and blood Rechabites to be found somewhere today.

The last chapters of the book of Ezekiel are devoted to his visionary description of the Temple of God that will be present on earth when all things are restored to their pristine perfect conditions. Guess who will be found there? Levites! They will be administering various ecclesiastical functions in this perfect world. Several passages in Ezekiel attest to this fact. Consider Ezekiel 40:46 as an example: *" . . . these are the sons of Zadok among the sons of Levi, which come near to the LORD to minister unto him."* If there are sons of Levi that will be functioning in a ministerial capacity in the restored Kingdom of God, then they must certainly be in existence today!

Finding Levites in History

So, where should we look to find the genetic sons of Levi? Remembering that Levites were parceled out among all the other

Joseph of Arimathea in St. John's Chapel in Glastonbury, England.

tribes of Israel that they might be of greater service to the nation as a whole, it is almost certain that there are Levites to be found wherever Israelites have wandered through the many centuries. Perhaps many of the ministers that have been called of God, who love the Bible, who are committed to Jesus Christ, are genetically descended from Levi. Maybe some of the great preachers and teachers of God's truth were Levites: men like Martin Luther, John Calvin, George Whitefield, John Wesley, and Charles Spurgeon. It is interesting to note that the proclivity for men to be drawn to become ministers or preachers seems to run in families. It is plausible that these families are, in fact, of Levitic descent.

However, there is one branch of the Levitical family tree that can be traced through history with great confidence. Through a series of providential marriages, the Levitic line merged with the Davidic dynasty. Several infusions of priestly genetics enriched the Davidic genealogy. Since the family tree of the royal Davidic line has been preserved in Scripture up to the time of Christ, and secular historic records pick it up from that point until now, we can also find the Levite present.

The current royal family of England is not only the literal, genetic offspring of the seed of David, but is also the literal, genetic offspring of at least one branch of Levi. Thus, when Scripture states that the lawgiver will be between the feet of Judah (Genesis 49:10), it is speaking in an almost literal sense! The Levitic priesthood is found within the loins of the monarchs of England!

Caractacus, the warrior king of the British, who when taken to Rome as a prisoner, helped establish Christianity in the city of Rome.

At the end of this chapter, a list of every person in this long genealogy spanning three thousand years is available for review. It is interesting to note that several kings in the Davidic line were also linchpin people in the history of our faith. One of them was Solomon (circa 980 B.C.), the builder of the great temple. He inherited the Levitic bloodline from his mother Bathsheba, who was of the priestly line of her father Ammiel. Another was Caradoc or Caractacus (circa 90 A.D.), a king of ancient Britain. He was a Levite through Anna the daughter of Joseph of Arimathea who was of the priestly line of Matthat. Caractacus helped introduce Christianity in both Britain and the city of Rome. Yet another was Constantine the Great (circa A.D. 325), a direct descendant of Caractacus through his mother. Constantine legalized Christianity in the Roman Empire and presided over the famous and important Council of Nicea.

Constantine, of Levitic descent, the Emperor who legalized Christianity throughout the Roman Empire in 313 A.D.

His mother Helena personally sponsored research that identified most of the key locations of important events in the Holy Land.

A bit more recent, Henry VIII (circa A.D. 1535) broke with the corrupt Roman Catholic Church and established the independent Church of England. He did so for selfish reasons, but the action nonetheless opened the door to the Protetstant Reformation in England and paved the way for a mighty spiritual revival in that nation. Henry was descended from Constantine and from the ancient Welsh kings, both branches of which go back to Joseph of Arimathea. Less than a century later in 1603, James I of England (James VI of Scotland) commissioned the translation of the King James Bible, the most widely used and reliable translation in the English language. The completion of this translation in 1611 ushered in the flowering of England's cultural renaissance. James was descended from Levi from several directions, through the same kings as Henry VIII, going back to Joseph of Arimathea as well as through the Scottish kings who directly flowed from Tea Tephi, the daughter of the last king of Judah, Zedekiah. He was in turn descended from Solomon, his mother Bathsheba, and her father Ammiel, of a priestly line.

The present members of the royal family, including Queen Elizabeth II, her eldest son and heir Charles, the Prince of Wales, and his eldest son, Prince William are all descendants of Levi. They are recipients of the covenant blessings of the Levitic Covenant. Any personal shortcomings present in their life do not negate the existence or the power of this covenant, for God works His providential ways through mortal men, despite being stained with the blemishes of sin.

Henry VIII, of the Tudor dynasty. Without intending to, he opened the door to spiritual revival in England.

It is important to remember that this is only one branch of the descendants of Levi in the earth today. Without doubt, there are many others shrouded in obscurity, some of whom are surely inclined to the calling of ministerial duty before God. They do not know they are Levites, but perhaps that is why they feel the compelling call of the Holy Spirit, driving them into the direct service of Christ as leaders of His various flocks.

Now that we have identified the genetic sons of Levi in the royal family of England, we are able to see that the people of the West, that is, the Anglo-Saxons of England and their related people of the same genetic stock, are Israelites. They are not just "spiritual" Israelites, but the true physical offspring of the ancient Hebrews.

The Genealogical Table

For those who are interested, what follows is a list of names beginning with Abraham. This list forks at Levi, the son of Jacob from whom the Levitical priesthood descends. The reader can observe the direct descent, without interruption, of the line of priests from ancient times, through the classical and medieval

periods. It continues into the line of Welsh kings from whom is the descent of modern monarchs of Great Britain.

Most of the names are male however, the occasions of descent through a female are noted with an asterisk. This table is actually simplified, and there are more ways that Elizabeth II is a direct descendant of Levi than what is shown here. The names in bold print are individuals who made historic decisions of a religious nature that resonated through the centuries. Much of the information of this table was derived from

James I, who appointed the translation of the King James Bible.

the work of Dennis M. Whitney of Royal House Publishing, PO Box 2525, Van Nuys, California 91404.

1850 B.C.   Abraham
                             Isaac
                             Jacob
                             Levi

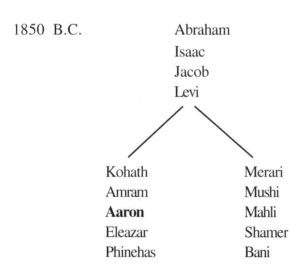

Kohath   Merari
Amram   Mushi
Aaron   Mahli
Eleazar   Shamer
Phinehas   Bani

Abishua	Amzi
Bukki	Hilkiah
Uzzi	Amaziah
Zerahiah	Hashabiah
Maraioth	Malluch
Azariah	Abdi
Amariah	Kishi
Ahitub	Ethan
Zadok	Obed-Edom
Ahimaaz	Ammiel
Azariah	Bathsheba*
Johanan	**Solomon** 985 B.C.
Azariah	Nathan
Amariah	Mattatha
Ahitub	Melea
Maraioth	Eliakim
Zadok	Jonan
Shallum	Joseph
Hilkiah	Judah
Azariah	Simon
Seraiah	Levi
Jehozadak	Matthat
Joshua	Joram
Jehoiakim	Eliezer
Eliashib	Jose
Joiada	Er
Johanan	Elmodam
Jadduah	Cosam
Onias	Addi
Simon	Melchi
daughter (name?)*	Neri
Joseph	Zerubabel
Johanna	Abiud

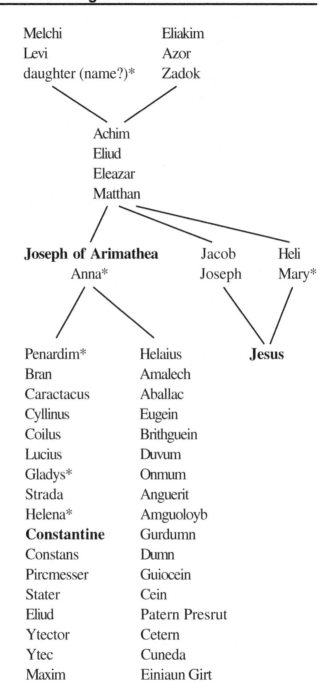

Melchi   Eliakim
Levi   Azor
daughter (name?)*   Zadok

                Achim
                Eliud
                Eleazar
                Matthan

Joseph of Arimathea   Jacob   Heli
        Anna*   Joseph   Mary*

Penardim*   Helaius   **Jesus**
Bran   Amalech
Caractacus   Aballac
Cyllinus   Eugein
Coilus   Brithguein
Lucius   Duvum
Gladys*   Onmum
Strada   Anguerit
Helena*   Amguoloyb
325 A.D. **Constantine**   Gurdumn
Constans   Dumn
Pircmesser   Guiocein
Stater   Cein
Eliud   Patern Presrut
Ytector   Cetern
Ytec   Cuneda
Maxim   Einiaun Girt

Dimet	Catgalaunlanhir
Nimet	Mailcun
Gloitguin	Run
Clotri	Beli
Trifun	Jacob
Aircol	Cadwan
Guertipir	Cadwallon
Cincar	Cadwallader
Petr	Edwal
Arthur	Roderick
Naugoy	Conan
Cloten	Esyith
Cathen	Roderick the Great 878 A.D.
Catgocaum	Anarawd
Regin	Idwal
Teudos	Meyrick
Margetuit	Idwal
Ovei	Jago
Tancoyst	Conan
Hymeyt	Gruffydh
Loumerc	Owain
Elen*	Iorworth
Owen	Llewellyn Fawr 1236 A.D.
Meredith	Gwyladus*
Anghered*	Roger Mortimer
Blethyn	Edmund Mortimer
Meredith	Roger Mortimer
Gruffydh	Edmund Mortimer
Owen	Roger Mortimer
Gruffydh	Edmund Mortimer
Llewellyn	Roger Mortimer
Eva*	Anne Mortimer*
Gwertil*	Richard of York

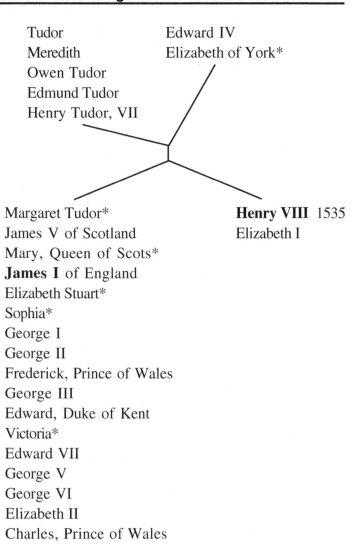

Tudor
Meredith
Owen Tudor
Edmund Tudor
Henry Tudor, VII

Edward IV
Elizabeth of York*

Margaret Tudor*
James V of Scotland
1588   Mary, Queen of Scots*
1611   **James I** of England
Elizabeth Stuart*
Sophia*
George I
George II
Frederick, Prince of Wales
1776   George III
Edward, Duke of Kent
Victoria*
Edward VII
George V
George VI
2013   Elizabeth II
Charles, Prince of Wales
William, Duke of Cambridge

Henry VIII 1535
Elizabeth I

8

Evidence from Genesis: Prophetic Utterences of Israel Fulfilled in History

*"History is a pact between
the dead, the living, and the yet unborn."*
–Edmund Burke

Prophecy is most assuredly a popular and intriguing theological topic. But a large portion of books on prophecy go far beyond Scripture and delve into titillating speculations, the great majority of which prove to be incorrect. In this essay, we shall avoid excessive speculation and deal with the words of Scripture, matching them with history, heraldry, and plain symbolism.

The earliest and perhaps the most complete set of prophecies regarding the twelve tribes was given before the tribes ever developed. In Genesis 49, Jacob offered a series of prophetic comments to his twelve sons while on his deathbed. In verse 1, Jacob specifically says to his sons that these are the things *"which shall befall you in the last days."* These insightful predictions run parallel to Deuteronomy 33, which contains a series of prophetic blessings that Moses gave to the twelve tribes just before his death. Moses' comments are not identical to Jacob's, but nonetheless bear many profound similarities. A correlation of these two chapters will provide some extremely useful insights into the identification of the Israelite tribes in the modern world. Let us begin, taking each tribe according to the birth order of the twelve sons as recorded in Genesis 29-30 and analyzing the comments of Jacob in Genesis 49.

Reuben: Strong and Dignified, but Unstable

Reuben is the eldest of Jacob's twelve sons. Of Reuben, Jacob said this: *"Thou art my firstborn, my might, and the beginning of my strength, the excellency of dignity, and the*

France has a long history of both licentiousness and political instability.

excellency of power: Unstable as water, thou shalt not excel; because thou wentest up to thy father's bed; then defilest thou it: he went up to my couch" (Genesis 49:3-4). The preliminary assessment of Reuben sounds very commendable: a strong man of dignity and power. But the subsequent prediction is sobering indeed; he was unable to excel because of an innate unstable nature, most notoriously exhibited when he engaged in a sexual liaison with Bilhah, Rachel's handmaid, his father's concubine, and his half-brothers' mother. Reuben appears to have real virtue, but an inability to control his passions.

Reuben is most closely associated on a national scale in recent centuries with France. France has always been a nation with many fine qualities, rich in cultural and intellectual resources. Yet, it has a tendency toward political instability. Prosperity and great potential are repeatedly undercut by tumultuous revolutions and changes in government. France has often been only one short step away from European or even global dominance, yet has never quite closed the gap. Furthermore, the French are famous for their sexually libertine habits, another connection to their forebear, Reuben.

Simeon and Levi: the Scattered Ones

Jacob prophesies about his second and third sons together, Simeon and Levi. Of them he stated, *"Simeon and Levi are brethren; instruments of cruelty are in their habitations. O my soul, come not thou into their secret; unto their assembly, mine honor, be not thou united: for in their anger they slew a man, and in their selfwill they digged down a wall. Cursed be their anger, for it was fierce; and their wrath, for it was cruel: I will divide them in Jacob, and scatter them in Israel"* *(Genesis 49:5-7)*. The singular event that figured large in the lives of Jacob's family involving these two brothers was the destruction of the city of Shechem. Simeon and Levi plotted and carried out a terrible revenge for the seduction of their sister Dinah (Genesis 34). Jacob was highly displeased with this revenge and these two sons. Jacob discerned a streak of cruelty in them that he predicted would be found in their descendants and would prove to be the agent of their scattering within Israel.

It is easy to identify Levi's scattering. It was providential and, oddly enough, a result of his selection as the priestly tribe. Moses saw virtues in Levi and stated, *"They shall teach Jacob thy judgments and Israel thy law . . . Bless, LORD, his substance, and accept the work of his hands"* *(Deuteronomy 33:10-11)*. Levi was intentionally spread throughout the other tribes of Israel to serve in priestly roles. The scattering of Simeon is less well established, although clues exist. Simeon is the only tribe that Moses did not give any prophecy about in Deuteronomy 33. Evidently, as early as Moses' time, Simeon was already showing signs of being absorbed into the other tribes. We know that this did occur shortly after the time of the Israelites settling the land of Canaan. Nonetheless, Simeon does have a modern nation associated with him: Spain. Spain has a reputation of notable cruelty, just as Simeon did. Consider the Spanish colonial system, the Spanish Inquisition, and the national sport of Spain, bullfighting. The Spanish people have always tended to marry into whatever local population they find themselves, thus fulfilling the prophetic tendency toward scattering.

Judah: the Great Warriors

The fourth born son of Jacob was Judah, who like his three elder brothers was of Leah. One of the most remarkable of the

Coat of arms of the Kingdom of Hanover, Germany.

brood, Judah, was praised by his father: *"Judah, thou art he whom thy brethren shall praise: thy hand shall be in the neck of thy enemies; thy father's children shall bow down before thee. Judah is a lion's whelp: from the prey, my son, thou art gone up: he stooped down, he couched as a lion, and as an old lion; who shall rouse him up? The sceptre shall not depart from Judah, nor a lawgiver from between his feet, until Shiloh come; and unto him shall the gathering of the people be. Binding his foal unto the vine, and his ass's colt unto the choice vine; he washed his garments in wine, and his clothes in the blood of grapes: His eyes shall be red with wine, and his teeth white with milk"* (Genesis 49:8-12). Two themes present themselves in this passage. The more prominent is the powerful, predatory nature of Judah. Phrases like, *"neck of thy enemies . . . lion's whelp . . . who shall rouse him up . . . blood of grapes . . . eyes red with wine"* all profile a warlike, frightening image. Thus, to identify Judah among modern nations, we should search among those people who are prone to warfare. The second theme is sandwiched in the center of the passage: rulership. *"The sceptre shall not depart from Judah"* is a key indicator of royalty. What nation has spawned much royalty?

The German people of central Europe are the modern representatives of Judah. What modern nation has been as warlike, frightening, and militaristic as Germany? For two centuries, Germany has used its military prowess to conquer and forge its way in the world. In the twentieth century it took the combined weight of Britain, France, Russia, and the United States to keep Germany in its box.

With respect to rulership, the most important royal family in the world today, the British House of Windsor, is most decidedly quite German. Just a few short decades ago, the *Windsors* were known to the world as the *Mountbattens*. But they only obtained that label when World War I erupted and they did not want to be known as the very German sounding *Battenbergs* (Mountbatten is merely the English form of Battenberg). But going back a bit further, we discover that the royal family was called the *House of Hannover*.

Note the three lions of the British royal coat of arms.

Why? Because in the early 1700s the royal House of Hannover was invited to rule over the British nation. They have been ruling ever since! Indeed, many of the

European royal families of the last several hundred years have been remarkably German in their genetics. One final observation emphasizes this: what is the dominant heraldic symbol among European royalty? The lion. Lions of sundry designs are everywhere upon European royal crests. Indeed, the most familiar royal crest is that of the Plantagenets, who ruled England for four hundred years. What is it? Three lions. Why three? Because there are three lions mentioned in Genesis 49:9. Count them and allow yourself the luxury of being amazed at the prophetic power of Scripture!

Dan: Militant Troublemakers

Jacob's next son was Dan, born of Rachel's handmaid Bilhah. Of Dan, Jacob prophesied: *"Dan shall judge his people, as one of the tribes of Israel. Dan shall be a serpent by the way, an adder in the path, that biteth the horse heels, so that his rider shall fall backward" (Genesis 49:16-17).* From

One of several white horses from pre-Roman Britain, a mark of the trailblazing, migratory tribe of Dan.

these comments we see two elements. First, Dan would be a leader among his tribal brethren, which is positive. A *judge* was a military leader in ancient Israel, and this term should be taken as an indicator of military power. But secondly, and negatively, Dan would be a trouble-maker. The imagery of a serpent striking at a horse and dismounting the rider can only be construed as most unhelpful! Perhaps Samson's life can be used to illustrate how these two elements of Dan can come together. Samson was a powerful leader in Israel from the tribe of Dan, but his personal weaknesses brought war and avenging

Philistines down on the Israelites time and again. Finally, his reckless ways caught up with him, and he was captured, never to be free again. He was a fearsome warrior, but one so headstrong that his potential was limited.

The symbols of the tribe of Dan are a horse and a serpent. Dan is known as being a tribe of adventurers, trailblazers that were often far out ahead of the other tribes in their migratory treks. Many place names in Europe show the trail of Dan, finally culminating in the nation of Denmark. But this small country is only a fraction of Dan's greater influence. Danes, or Danites, settled in the early medieval period in many other portions of Europe, not the least of which was northern England, which was for a long time simply called Danelaw. This Danite element of the English population eventually made their way to America and figured prominently in the American Revolution. This is why the most popular banner of the American War of Independence was a serpent emblazoned with the words, "Don't tread on me." Of course, from the British point of view, such American colonists were nothing more than rebels of the worst sort, which helps explain how Jacob's original prophecy of Dan could have seemingly contradictory positive and negative elements!

A popular banner from the American Revolution.

Naphtali: Like a Deer

Following Dan, Bilhah bore Nahphtali. Jacob's deathbed prophecies regarding Naphtali are exceedingly brief: *"Naphtali is a hind let loose, he giveth goodly words"* (Genesis 49:21). From this terse commentary we can only conclude the barest of facts. The prophecy is positive; his descendants will have an ability to communicate well. The symbol of the tribe is a hind—a female deer. Norway is the modern nation most closely associated with Naphtali.

Gad: Active in War and Religion

The next son of Jacob was Gad, this time born by Zilpah, Leah's handmaid. Again, Jacob said little about another of his middle sons: *"Gad, a troop shall overcome him, but he shall overcome at the last" (Genesis 49:19).* However, in this case, Moses' prophetic vision adds some useful clues: *"Blessed be he that enlargeth Gad: he dwelleth as a lion, and teareth*

The actor Rex Harrison in a portrayal of Giuliano della Rovere, Pope Julius II. This renaissance pope typified the militant aspirations of the papacy.

the arm with the crown of the head. And he provideth the first part for himself, because there, in a portion of the lawgiver, was he seated; and he came with the heads of the people, he executed the justice of the LORD, and his judgments with Israel" Deuteronomy 33:20-21). It can be clearly seen that Gad will exercise dominion, particularly in law and justice. There is a warlike element, *"dwelleth as a lion,"* and *"teareth the arm."* But there is also a religious element, *"lawgiver,"* remembering that all law is religious in nature and the term *lawgiver* in the Bible is a priestly function. What nation in history has a long record encompassing both of these elements? Italy. When thinking of war and law, think of Rome: Roman law and Roman justice. When thinking of religious leadership and religious law, think of the Papacy, centered at Rome for over a thousand years. Italy is an excellent fulfillment of the prophecies regarding Gad.

Asher: Peaceful and Prosperous

Asher came next, also born of Zilpah. Jacob's prophecy of Asher is brief, but quite positive: *"Out of Asher his bread shall be fat, and he shall yield royal dainties" (Genesis 49:20).* Moses made comments that run similar: *"Let Asher be blessed with children; let him be acceptable to his brethren, and let him dip his foot in oil" (Deuteronomy 33:24).* The tenor of these words indicates prosperity, growth, and relative tranquility. Sweden is the nation most closely associated with Asher. Certainly twentieth century Sweden reflects these comments very well, for Sweden avoided both world wars and the ferocious destruction thereof. Meanwhile, the Swedes steadily developed one of the highest living standards in the world and are well known for the production of high quality items.

Issachar: Caught between Burdens

It turns out that Leah was not finished bearing children after all, for she had another son, Issachar. This ninth son of Jacob did not enjoy a particularly cheerful prophecy from his father's lips: *"Issachar is a strong ass couching down between two burdens: And he saw that the rest was good, and the land that it was pleasant; and he bowed his shoulder to bear, and became a servant unto tribute" (Genesis 49:14).* It appears that Issachar's latter days were to be profiled by a plodding, stoic acceptance of either one burden or the other, neither one, however, to be so oppressive as to be unbearable. What nation typifies this? Actually, two do, and their situation is almost identical. First, consider Finland. Its history is characterized by domination coming from either the Russians or the Swedes. Both have exploited and beat up on the steady, patient Finns. Second, Poland fits well also. In the case of the Poles, they have suffered a long train of abuse from either the Russians or the Germans. Their affliction from the Russians and

Germans dates back nearly a thousand years. Both Finland and Poland have long been squashed between East and West; their history and culture reflect this.

Zebulon: the Seafarers

Leah gave Jacob yet another son, Zebulon. Of him Jacob prophesied, *"Zebulon shall dwell at the haven of the sea; and he shall be for an haven of ships: and his border shall*

be unto Zidon" (Genesis 49:13). Zidon was located on the coast of Canaan and was equipped with an excellent harbor, enabling Zebulon to partly fulfill the prophecy in ancient times. Yet latter day Zebulon also fulfills this maritime quality with excellent harbors of its own and it own sea-going traditions. Moses foresaw this and stated that Zebulon would *"suck of the abundance of the seas, and of treasures hid in the sands" (Deuteronomy*

A seventeenth century ship like the Dutch possessed. As did Zebulon, the Dutch looked to the sea for their future.

33:19). Holland best represents Zebulon among modern Israelite nations. Although small, Holland has always looked to the sea for wealth and opportunity, even draining shallow ocean beds to provide living space. For hundreds of years the Dutch East India Company successfully enriched this small nation by importing products from the Spice Islands of Southeast Asia to markets in Europe and elsewhere. Later, the Dutch developed petroleum resources from the North Sea and Indonesian islands which fueled their economy. Truly, Holland fits the prophetic pattern well.

Joseph: the Empire Builders

Jacob's eleventh son was delivered to him by his beloved Rachel, who finally bore a child of her own flesh. This was Joseph, the most remarkable of Jacob's sons, the one who received the double blessing of Reuben's forfeited birthright. Not surprisingly, Jacob had a great deal of good things to say about Joseph: *"Joseph is a fruitful bough, even a fruitful bough by a well; whose branches run over the wall: The archers have sorely grieved him, and shot at him, and hated him: But his bow abode in strength, and the arms of his hands were made strong by the hands of the mighty God of Jacob; (from thence is the shepherd, the stone of Israel:) Even by the God of thy father, who shall help thee; and by the Almighty, who shall bless thee with blessings of heaven above, blessings of the deep that lieth under, blessings of the breasts, and of the womb: The blessings of thy father have prevailed above the blessings of my progenitors unto the utmost bounds of the everlasting hills: they shall be on the head of Joseph, and on the crown of the head of him that was separate from his brethren"* *(Genessis 49:22-26).*

This language informs us that Joseph will be successful in war, will have a large population that expands beyond its original homelands, and although he will have enemies, he will not notably suffer from their attacks. Moses saw wealth from the earth in Joseph's future: *"Blessed of the Lord be his land, for the precious things of heaven, for the dew, and for the deep that coucheth beneath, And for the precious fruits brought forth by the sun, and for the precious things put forth by the moon, And for the chief things of the ancient mountains, and for the precious things of the lasting hills . . ."* *(Deuteronomy 33:13-15).* Do you see the agricultural abundance, the success in mining operations, and the derivation of wealth from the oceans?

But that is not all. Moses also foresaw colonial expansion and empire: *"His glory is like the firstling of his bullock, and his horns are like the horns of unicorns: with them he shall push the people together to the ends of the earth: and they are the ten thousands of Ephraim and the thousands of Manasseh"* (*Deuteronomy 33:17*). What a blessing is upon Joseph: wealth, a large population, global empire, honor! What nation could this be in modern world?

A nineteenth century poster glorifying the expansion of the British Empire.

There is only one people that can fit this description—the English speaking people who have expanded from their modest island home of England to dominate the planet, like no others ever have. Between the mother nation of England and her daughters America, Australia, Canada, and elsewhere, the English people produce more, have more, rule more, and in general dominate much of our planet. And this has been true now for three hundred years! Who feeds the world corn, wheat, and other foodstuffs? The English-speaking sons of Joseph. Who has mined the deepest gold mines from the hills, drilled the deepest oil wells at the bottom of the oceans, and sent their armies to police the four corners of the world? The English-speaking sons of Joseph. The sun never set on the British Empire, and now America manages all the world's problems. Just as Joseph was the problem solver when the ancient world suffered from famine, so are Joseph's sons the problem solvers when the modern world experiences a crisis.

Benjamin: the Opportunists

The last of Jacob's sons was Benjamin, also of Rachel. In this lad, Jacob foresaw an opportunist: *"Benjamin shall ravin as a wolf: in the morning he shall devour the prey, and at night he shall divide the spoil" (Genesis 49:27).* What modern nation has a history of opportunistic development? Iceland. This Norse people settled on this marginal island hundreds of years ago looking for a fresh start, a new beginning. They were renowned as raiders, explorers, a seafaring people who lived from the plunder they took from others. Little brother Benjamin was always a small tribe in ancient Israel and is a small nation today; but they have been a fierce bunch, brawling their way along through the centuries.

There you have it: the twelve sons of Jacob, fulfilling their aged father's visions for the future, embodied in the modern nations of Caucasian Europe. If you are descended from one of these nations, then you are an Israelite, and your heritage is found among these prophecies. What a rich legacy you have!

9

An Eschatological Perspective: Israel Is the Focus of Bible Prophecy

"What we look for does not come to pass.
God finds a way for what none foresaw."
–Euripides

The greatest single help in unlocking the prophetic portions of Scripture is this simple concept: the Church, the body of Christ, is constituted from ethnic Israel. This straightforward idea avoids the tangled web of prophetic gymnastics that enmesh most expositors of Bible prophecy.

If you were to survey all of the books that have been published in the area of eschatology within the last century, a bewildering array of opinons would overwhelm you. Unlike many aspects of theology, there is no consensus among biblical scholars regarding what will occur at the end of the age. Indeed, there are virtually no areas of overlapping agreement on any facet of end-time events or personalities.

Eschatology has become a popular subject in recent decades. The uncertainty of our times and a general sense that affairs in our society are amiss in profound ways propels many Bible students to search for answers. A great many writers have cashed in on this anxiety and have written much, even novels, that make eschatological assumptions like the existence of the bodily rapture. But virtually all of them are failing to recognize the single most vital truth about eschatology: the Church, the body of Christ, is derived from ethnic Israel.

The Dilemma

Without this framework of truth, that is, the church and Israel are one and the same, a fundamental problem immediately emerges. Virtually all of Bible prophecy deals with Israel. Daniel, Revelation, Ezekiel 36-39, Zechariah 14, and other portions of Scripture central to prophecy are all oriented on an axis about Israel. Israel is the focus of prophecy. Few, if any, passages deal with the church outside of an Israelite context. How is this a dilemma?

If you presume that those commonly referred to as the Jews today represent the bulk of biblical Israel, you have a problem. Where does the "Gentile" church fit in to God's prophetic plan? Prophetic passages are silent concerning the future role of a "Gentile" church. Yet, they cannot be left out! After all, it is the church that has carried the gospel of Jesus Christ to the ends of the earth. It is the church that has made the Bible available to anyone who wishes to read its pages. It is the church that has written the profound confessions of faith, sung the inspiring hymns, built the soaring cathedrals, and done virtually every other great Christian labor over the past two thousand years. And what people have done all of this in the name of Jesus Christ? It is the Caucasian people of Western Europe. They have borne the burdens, carried the load, and suffered for the cause of Christ. Anyone with a working knowledge of church history knows this is the truth. What they may not know is that Israelites are the people who make up the church!

Meanwhile, what have the Jews done for the cause of Christ? Virtually nothing. In fact, many repudiate His name and dishonor His redemptive sacrifice.

Yet Scripture plainly indicates that the vast bulk of Bible prophecy revolves around the central axis of Israel. Does this mean that the non-Christian Jews are going to be the central focus of God's rewards in prophecy while the Caucasian church of historic Christianity, who has upheld His name and reputation for two thousand years, is left out of God's prophetic blessings? Well, of course, that makes no sense! What kind of God would deal so unjustly? But that is exactly the dilemma facing modern

The Woman of Revelation 12

theologians who insist that the people called the Jews represent the bulk of biblical Israel, and the historic church of Western Europe is just an energetic mass of non-Israelite converts.

There is, however, an exceedingly straightforward solution. Simply recognize that the ethnic people of Western Europe are indeed biblical Israel in a genetic sense. Acknowledge that the prophetic passages dealing with Israel are relevant to the historic Christian church that blossomed for centuries in Caucasian Europe, and later America. Such an admission resolves all prophetic tension! Now, God's prophetic plan of preserving Israel, nurturing Israel, and rewarding Israel is just and proper, for it is true ethnic Israel that has been faithful to the cause of Christ, enduring under difficult times, and zealous to press forward the name of Jesus Christ!

Take a look at Revelation chapter 12. This chapter reveals that the church is made up of ethnic Israel. Notice verses 1-2: *"And there appeared a great wonder in heaven; a woman clothed with the sun, and the moon under her feet, and upon her head a crown of twelve stars: And she being with child cried, travailing in birth, and pain to be delivered."*

This woman can be none other than ethnic Israel; the twelve crowns are the key indicator. The child brought forth under great historic duress was Jesus Christ, born into the oppression of cruel Roman occupation. Continue by reading verses 5-6: *"And she brought forth a man child, who was to rule all nations with a rod of iron: and her child was caught up unto God, and to his throne. And the woman fled into the wilderness, where she had a place prepared of God . . ."* The man child destined to someday rule all nations is again Christ, who did indeed ascend into heaven. Meanwhile, the woman, Israel, found safety in the wilderness parts of the earth. Is that not an excellent description of the Nordic Israelites who had migrated into the wilds of northwest Europe and then later to America? Resume at the end of the chapter, verse 17: *"And the dragon was wroth with the woman, and went to make war with the remnant of her seed, which keep the commandments of God, and have the testimony of Jesus Christ."* The dragon is Satan. And with whom is he angry? The woman, who is Israel. And what are the hallmarks of her remaining descendants? They keep God's commandments and adhere to the gospel of Jesus Christ. Does this description fit the people commonly referred to as the Jews? It absolutely does not. They openly reject Jesus Christ; neither are they famous for keeping God's commandments, for it is many of them that are eager to take down Ten Commandment plaques in our public places. But who does fit this description? Is it not the remaining faithful among the Christian West, almost all of whom are ethnic Europeans, the descendants and inheritors of two thousand years of Christian culture? Without question, they are true Israelites. They are the genetic offspring of the woman. They are the people around whom the vast bulk of biblical prophecy swirls. They are the apple of God's eye (Deuteronomy 32:9-10). Meanwhile, who are the people known today as the Jews? They have taken an identity that does not belong to them, and God has strong words about this stolen identity (see Revelation 2:9 and 3:9).

Because Bible prophecy deals almost exclusively with Israel, and because most modern expositors of Bible prophecy refuse to acknowledge that the Caucasian Christian West is indeed Israel, they must deal with the problem that the historic church has been left out of God's prophetic plan. That being obviously unjust, they have been forced to come up with creative solutions to "fit in" the church. There are three main approaches to this problem. Let us consider each of them, for all three are a real stretch of biblical hermeneutics. Admitting that the historic church has been made up of ethnic Israel would be so much easier!

Proposed Theological Solutions

The first so-called solution is generally referred to as dispensationalism. There are many varieties of dispensationalism, but they all boil down to this common thread: God has two pathways by which eternal life in the kingdom of God can be obtained. "Gentiles" are saved by faith in Jesus Christ, and "Jews" are brought into the kingdom through exciting prophetic events that provide a special dispensation by which they gain access to God, for after all, they are "God's chosen people." Dispensationalism is a two-track eschatology, one for "Jews" and another for "Gentiles." The Israeli state established in 1948 is viewed as fulfillment of Israel's prophesied re-gathering. A good Bible student, however, knows this is impossible, for Ezekiel 37:11-14 makes it plain that there will be no regathering without the

John Nelson Darby, the father of dispensationalism.

resurrection of the dead. And unless you are a preterist (they will be treated later), you will be able to obviously perceive that the resurrection of the dead has not occurred! Dispensationalism has become popular in recent decades, but it has borne little fruit and must constantly reinvent itself. For example, one popular dispensationalist proclaimed loudly in the 1970s that the "terminal generation" was now on earth since the 1948 regime was established. Well, a biblical generation is forty years, and since 1948 we are over sixty years and still counting!

The second attempt to find a place to "fit in" the church is called amillennialism. Again, there are different stripes of

amillennialists, but they all hold this general thought in common: they believe that all of the prophecies pertaining to Israel are not to be taken too literally, but should be viewed as figurative language. This then allows the amillennialist the elasticity to stretch these prophecies considerably. They then claim that all of these prophecies have been transferred to the church. They do this without acknowledging that the church is really made up of Israel. This cession, or transfer, of prophetic promises, is called

Origen, the third century Alexandrian scholar, popularized amillenialism.

supercessionism. In a nutshell, they claim that the church is spiritual Israel, and we are headed for a spiritual kingdom. What are the problems with this theory? Foremost, there is no biblical authority for such a transfer—not a single verse (not to mention no need). Second, they must essentially discard giant sections of Scripture with a sweep of the hand as allegorical figurative language, which truly mutilates the obvious meaning of the text. The multitudinous prophecies regarding Israel are nationalistic in nature, and they just do not honestly make sense without that element. Amillennialism is not a new theory. But its weakness is what stimulated the rise of dispensationalism and also preterism, our next flawed eschatological scheme.

Preterism is the least convincing for those with a sound biblical worldview. It rejects many of the most basic precepts of historic Christianity including the creeds of the early church. Preterists purport that all Bible prophecy has been completely fulfilled. Yes, they believe that every last bit of it was fulfilled by A.D. 70 when the Romans destroyed Jerusalem. Their theory suggests that all of those prophecies about Israel were wrapped up and completed by A.D. 70 after which God started all over with a Gentile church. This may sound reasonable to the uninformed, but it is grossly irresponsible and dishonest to the integrity of Scripture. For example, the preterists must insist that the resurrection of the dead has occurred and we are now living in the fullness of the kingdom of God. Yes sir, this is it! This is as good as it gets!

The Simplest Solution Is the Correct One

All three approaches to resolve the tension—dispensationalism, amillennialism, and preterism—fail. The simplest solution is to acknowledge that the historic church of Caucasian Europeans is made up of ethnic Israel. This key will unlock the pages of Scripture and cast a new light on prophetic passages that have been hitherto unfathomable. May your quest of truth as you examine Bible prophecy be blessed by the God of Abraham, Isaac, and Jacob.

10

Objections to the Anglo-Israel Thesis Considered

*"The criterion of truth is that it works
even if nobody is prepared to acknowledge it."*
–Ludwig von Mises

Scripture and history offer, in this writer's humble opinion, abundant, indeed, virtually overwhelming evidence that the Caucasian race is the literal, physical offspring of the ancient Hebrews. Arguments abound in favor of the idea that the northern ten tribes of Israel migrated into Western Europe hundreds of years prior to the time of Christ, following their deportation from their Palestine homeland by the Assyrian Empire. Despite the copious evidence, however, many are reluctant to embrace the idea.

The most common negative reaction is not factually based from Scripture or history, but is purely an emotional, visceral attack. Usually the terms *racist*, *bigot*, or *hate-monger* are quickly launched without any actual substantive argument to back up such charges. It is presumed that this will immediately shut down further debate, and it sometimes does so. But if it does end the discussion, it does not do so by disproving the thesis on any intellectual basis, but merely by intimidating the proponent of the Anglo-Israel thesis into silence. Such intimidation and name-calling tactics are unjust, ignorant, and low-class.

Fortunately, in the long run, it is also ineffective, for truth has a way of continually resurfacing. The purpose of this article is not to respond to those who use shallow name-calling tactics. They are more prejudiced against open discussion than those whom they accuse. The goal here is to consider the arguments of those who raise honest, honorable objections.

The most common honest objections can be generally grouped into five categories. Each of these we shall consider in their turn.

Objection #1: Scripture Versus History

Objection Stated: Scripture trumps history because historically based arguments can be manipulated. Thus, historically based arguments are irrelevant and should not be considered.

Answer: Indeed, Scripture does trump history, for as Christians we accept by faith that the Bible is without error. That being said, however, Scripture has to be interpreted correctly, and it is quite plain that there are many, many different interpretations of the Bible on many, many different topics—resulting in massive confusion and disarray in the Christian world. One does not have to search very hard to find multiple examples of Scripture being manipulated and twisted by those who do so either through plain ignorance, their own intellectual blindness, or blatant deception for selfish reasons.

Certainly, history has potential for manipulation since facts have to be collected by archaeologists, linguists, and scholars and then collated by competent historians into a readable record. However, to simply brush history off in a casual manner is intellectually irresponsible. There is far more controversy in biblical interpretation than there is in history. That is to say, the level of confusion and debate over interpreting the Bible correctly is far greater than the effort to correctly identify the facts of history. With the exception of politically charged topics in the last century, historians have done a better job in their craft than theologians have done in theirs.

This is not to suggest that we use only history and then force-fit Scripture as a last minute thought. No, we must keep the Bible pre-eminent in our minds, and let history act as a check to see if our interpretation of Scripture is consistent with the real world. Ideally, Scriptural interpretation and historic facts should correlate one with the other. The Kingdom Israel thesis meets this test admirably. It is biblically sound and smoothly fits with known facts of ancient history. To suggest that history should be bypassed altogether as a vehicle to discover truth is an unintelligent, doltish proposal.

Objection #2: The Great Commission

Objection Stated: Since Jesus plainly stated that His followers were to go preach the gospel in all nations, all races and peoples must be the same in God's eyes, and it is irrelevant who the descendants of Israel might be today.

Answer: The reason that Jesus commanded His followers to *"Go ye therefore, and teach all nations"* *(Matthew 28:19)* and *"Go ye into all the world, and preach the gospel to every creature"* *(Mark 16:15)* is because ancient Israel was to be scattered among all nations. Since we

The Great Commission: commonly misunderstood

are not going to take the gospel to every dog and cat, we cannot sensibly interpret *"every creature"* in its most literal sense. So, in what sense do we take these two verses, known affectionately as the Great Commission?

Let us consider the context of Old Testament prophecy and fact. A repeated warning to the ancient Israelites was that God would scatter them among other nations and destroy their national identity if they continued to worship other gods. This is what was prophesied and indeed occurred: *"I will scatter thee among the heathen, and disperse thee in the countries, and will consume thy filthiness out of thee" (Ezekiel 22:15). "Son of man, when the house of Israel dwelt in their own land, they defiled it by their own way and doings . . . wherefore I poured my fury upon them for the blood they had shed upon the land, and for their idols wherewith they had polluted it: and I scattered them among the heathen, and they were dispersed through the countries: according to their way and according to their doings I judged them" (Ezekiel 36:17-19).* That was the bad news. The good news is that God also used the prophets to hold out a future hope and expectation that someday God would regather some of the scattered Israelites from the lands of their dispersion back into the land of Israel: *"And I will gather the remnant of my flock out of all countries whither I have driven them, and will bring them again to their folds, and they shall be fruitful and increase" (Jeremiah 23:3). "For lo, I will command, and I will sift the house of Israel among all nations, like as corn is sifted in a sieve, yet shall not the least grain fall upon the earth . . . And I will bring again the captivity of my people of Israel, and they shall build the waste cities, and inhabit them; and they plant vineyards, and drink the wine thereof; they shall also make gardens, and eat the fruit of them. And I will plant them upon their land, and they shall no more be pulled up out of their land which I have given them, saith the LORD thy God" (Amos 9:9, 4-15).*

By the time of Jesus' ministry in the land of Galilee and Judea, the prophecies of Israel's scattering had been fulfilled hundreds of years before. However, the regathering had not. The Great Commission was the necessary planting of the Gospel seed among all of the Israelites in the many countries where they were sent and scattered. A remnant would respond to that Gospel seed and would be the subjects of God's regathering at a future point in time. That regathering has not yet occurred. (Why the regathering is still unfulfilled prophecy will be answered shortly.)

Earlier in His ministry, Jesus had plainly stated that His entire effort was focused only upon one targeted group: Israelites. *"But he answered and said, I am not sent but unto the lost sheep of the house of Israel" (Matthew 15:24).* This is confirmed quite plainly in Hebrews when we discover that it is only to the twelve tribes of Israel that God is going to make the New Covenant: *". . . Behold the days come, saith the LORD when I will make a new covenant with the house of Israel and the house of Judah: not according to the covenant that I made with their fathers in the day when I took them by the hand to lead them out of the land of Egypt; because they continued not in my covenant, and I regarded them not, saith the LORD. For this is the covenant that I will make with the house of Israel after those days, saith the LORD; I will put my laws into their mind, and write them in their hearts: and I will be to them a God, and they shall be to me a people" (Hebrews 8:8-10).* The Great Commission cannot be interpreted to mean opening the covenant to non-Israelites because that would be contradictory to this very specific, plain passage. Hebrews 8:8-10 plainly states that the New Covenant is with the two Houses of Israel alone—no one else!

What the Great Commission does mean is that if Christ's disciples were going to spread the Gospel to all the Israelites, they would have to go where the Israelites had gone. Since God had sent the Israelites into many nations all over the world, that is where Jesus' disciples would have to go to fulfill Jesus' directive. Going to *"all nations"* and *"preaching the gospel to every creature"* as Scripture states does not mean that every person in every nation is the target any more than dogs and cats in every nation are the target. (After all, they are creatures.) The Great Commission is simply stating that to be sure that every one of God's elect Israelites has the opportunity to hear the Gospel, a very thorough blanket approach is necessary. Like shooting a shotgun cartridge that has hundreds of pellets with the desire that a few pellets hit the intended target, so is the Great Commission. The Gospel seed is spread far and wide to cover everyone, everywhere to ensure that Israelites are not overlooked during the planting season.

Who the Israelites are today is thus highly relevant.

The fact that the Great Commission does not target every person on the planet does not mean that God has no plan or destiny for all of His creatures. God certainly loves all people whom He created and certainly is not unjust. We need not worry that God will condemn non-Israelites to hell unjustly. Why God selected Israel in the Old Testament is not for us to deduce. But we know that is the case. Why He continued with the same people in the New Covenant is again not for us to understand—but that is the case. The plain facts of Scripture are that God has a special relationship with Israel. What He will do with other peoples on the planet He has not revealed in Scripture, but we can surely be confident that He will not treat them with cruelty or injustice.

Objection #3: Spiritual Israel

Objection Stated: Since the New Covenant is made with Spiritual Israel and people of all races are eligible to become members of the New Covenant, it is irrelevant who the descendants of Israel might be today.

Answer: It is a vital principle of biblical hermeneutics that one allows the clear and unambiguous verses on a given topic help interpret those that are less clear and open to multiple interpretations. To those who do not know the Bible well, it may seem that the Great Commission verses are simple enough and easily understood to mean all races and peoples everywhere on the planet. But to the well-grounded Bible student, it is obvious that such an interpretation cannot be.

Hebrews 8:8-10, as previously quoted, is the most specific and clear passage in the Bible regarding the New Covenant. It tells us bluntly that the parties to the New Covenant are with genetic Israel. Although the terms and nature of the covenant are different, the parties involved are not: they clearly are Jehovah and the twelve tribes of Israel. This is unmistakable in verse 9: *"Not according to the covenant that I made with their fathers . . ."* Note this is the same family tree. Different terms, yes; but different people? No.

Did you know that the terms "spiritual Israel" or "spiritual Israelite" do not even appear in the Bible? This is a relatively new idea and is not found in Scripture. It is a concept that poor Bible teachers have wrongly wrangled out of passages taken from Saint Paul's writings. For example, many assume that Paul teaches this notion based on the *"adoption"* of non-Israelites into the New Covenant, thus making them "spiritual Israelites." Proponents of such a theory offer Ephesians 1:5 as evidence: *"Having predestinated us unto the adoption of children by Jesus Christ to himself, according to the good pleasure of his will."* But notice this passage does not identify the subjects of this adoption. Does Paul ever state whom the adoption is for? Fortunately, he does in Romans 9:3-4: *"For I could wish that myself were accursed from Christ for my brethren, my kinsman according to the flesh: Who are Israelites; to whom pertaineth the adoption, and the glory, and the covenants, and the giving of the law, and the service of God, and the promises."* There you have it in plain words: the adoption pertains to Israelites.

But, one might argue, since a natural born genetic Israelite was already part of the covenants of the Old Testament, why would he need to be adopted? The answer is actually found in the prophets, who tell us that God became so frustrated with His people Israel that He divorced the northern kingdom, the ten tribes that drifted deep into apostasy. Jehovah broke the covenant with them. They were physically cast away into foreign lands, as discussed earlier; but more importantly, they were covenantally cast away. Consider Isaiah 50:1, which reads*: "Thus saith the LORD, Where is the bill of your mother's divorcement,*

whom I have put away? Or which of my creditors is it to whom I have sold you? Behold, for your iniquities have ye sold yourselves, and for your trans- gressions is your mother put away." A second witness to this important decision

A wild olive tree

by Jehovah is found in Jeremiah 3:8: *"And I saw, when for all the causes whereby backsliding Israel committed adul- tery I had put her away, and given her a bill of divorce; yet her treacherous sister Judah feared not, but went and played the harlot also."* (See also Isaiah 54:5-6 and Hosea 1:9.)

It was the divorced Israelites who had been cast out into the nations that were, in the New Testament, given the opportunity to be adopted back in under the new terms of the New Covenant. This is the *"grafting"* of the *"wild olive"* into the *"natural branches"* in Romans 11:16-24. The natural olive was the two- tribed nation of Judah, of whom Paul was a part. Although God had been quite displeased with them at times, they had never been divorced. The wild olives were the ten-tribes that had been divorced some seven centuries previously and who had migrated into Europe, multiplied, and fragmented into a number of peoples now going by different names and speaking different languages. These Greeks, Romans, Britons, Gauls, Scythians, and so forth were eligible to be adopted or grafted back into covenant relationship with God. They did not become "spiritual Israelites." They had been real Israelites all along, but were lost in idolatry, identity, and indifference to the things of God.

Understanding that the Greeks were Israelites also helps us properly understand what Paul meant in Galatians 3:28: *"There is neither Jew nor Greek, there is neither bond nor free, there is neither male nor female: for ye are all one in Christ Jesus."* The tension that existed between the Jews (that is, the un-divorced nation of Judah) with the divorced Israelites sent into dispersion, of whom the dominant Greek peoples were a large part, was to be ended. Not only was God going to work among Judah, but also among divorced Israel. This is what Paul's ministry was about.

Since the New Covenant is only for Israelites, as are the adoption and the grafting in, it is thus highly relevant who Israel is today.

Objection #4: The Regathering of Israel

Objection Stated: The prophesied regathering of all twelve tribes occurred long ago in the days of Ezra and Nehemiah; thus, the Caucasian nations of Europe which developed subsequent to that regathering cannot be of Israelitish descent.

Answer: This is the argument made by Dr. David Baron, an Englishman, in an attempt to discredit the Anglo-Israel movement in Great Britain. It was published and made popular by Walter Martin in his well-known book *Kingdom of the Cults,* first published in 1965 with several subsequent editions. This was Martin's rebuttal to Herbert W. Armstrong's Worldwide Church of God, which believed that English-speaking Caucasians of Britain and the United States were genetic descendants of the ancient Israelites.

It is surprising that Martin, often well informed, embraced such a shallow argument in his effort to discredit the Kingdom Israel thesis. First, it is relatively easy to show that the re-gathering, which is profiled so highly in the Old Testament Prophets, could not possibly have been fulfilled under Ezra and Nehemiah. Second, even if it were the re-gathering as they envision it, it does not necessarily eliminate the possibility that other Israelites could be the progenitors of Caucasian Europeans.

Let us begin with the second thought. Assuming that all twelve tribes returned in 526 B.C., why is there clear evidence that large numbers of the northern ten tribes were elsewhere later? Baron himself admits this, stating, *"There is not the least possibility of doubt that many of the settlements of the diaspora in the time of our Lord, north, south, west, as well as east of Palestine, were made up of those who never returned to the land of their fathers since the time of the Assyrian and Babylonian exiles, and were not only descendants of Judah, as Anglo-Israelism ignorantly presupposes, but of all of the twelve tribes scattered abroad (James 1:1)"* (*Kingdom of the Cults*, p. 312). I could not agree more. Josephus, the acclaimed Jewish (true Hebrew) historian who lived in A.D. 70, wrote of the return of the exiles from Babylon and had this to say: *"And when these Jews had understood what piety the king had towards God, and what kindness he had toward Ezra, they were all greatly pleased; further, many of them took their effects with them, and came to Babylon, as very desirous of going down to Jerusalem; but then the entire body of the people of Israel remained in that country; so that there are but two tribes in Asia and Europe subject to the Romans, while the ten tribes are beyond the Euphrates until now, and are an immense multitude, and not to be estimated by numbers"* (*Jewish Antiquities*, Book 2:5:2:132-133).

Looking at the Bible, we get the clear sense that it was primarily, if not exclusively, members of the tribes of Judah and Benjamin that returned to Jerusalem in 526 B.C. Ezra 1:5 reads: ***"Then rose up chief of the fathers of Judah and Benjamin, and the priests, and the Levites, with all them whose spirit God had raised, to go up to build the house of the Lord which is in Jerusalem."*** After their return, we discover that enemies rose up against them: ***"Now when the adversaries of Judah and Benjamin heard that the children of the captivity builded the temple . . ."*** *(Ezra 4:1)*. Notice that it was against the tribes of Judah and Benjamin that enemies of God rose up.

Rebuilding the Temple under Ezra, by Dore'. Some mistakenly assert that this was the prophesied regathering of all twelve tribes.

The insistence of Baron and Martin that substantial quantities of *all twelve tribes* returned is thus unlikely. They cite the fact that Anna was of the tribe of Asher some five hundred years later in the days of Jesus (Luke 2:36). Perhaps there were *some* of other tribes that returned with Judah and Benjamin, but nowhere in Scripture is it so stated. It is more likely that Anna was a descendant of the poor remnant of the land that was never taken away to Assyria or Babylon. That a few did remain is recorded in 2 Kings 24:14:

"And he [Nebuchadnezzar] *carried away all Jerusalem, and all the princes, and all the mighty men of valour, even ten thousand captives, and all the craftsmen and smiths: none remained, save the poorest sort of the people of the land."*

It is thus clear from Scripture and history that the great bulk of the ten tribes did not return in 526 B.C. and remained dispersed among the nations of the then-known world. What happened to them? Baron and Martin have no answer. But the Anglo-Israel thesis does.

Now to the first part of their theory, namely, that the return in Ezra's time was the regathering spoken of by the Prophets. Even if all twelve tribes were present with Ezra and Nehemiah, which has been shown to be implausible, it still could not be the fulfillment of prophecy. Baron cites Ezekiel chapter 37 as the prophetic text of choice. That is fine, but apparently Baron did not read this chapter very thoroughly.

In verse 24 we find that David was to be their king: *"And David my servant shall be king over them . . . "* That never occurred, even if we assume this is meant to mean one of David's descendants would rule. For several hundred years after Ezra's return, the little nation of Judah never had a king. When they finally did establish the Maccabean (Hasmonean) dynasty, it was not of David's house. David's house was languishing in obscurity but was finally used when Jehovah plucked up Joseph the carpenter to be the father of Jesus (see Matthew 1).

A second problem for Baron emerges in Ezekiel 37, his prophetic chapter of choice, when the reader reaches verse 25: *"And they shall dwell in the land that I have given Jacob my servant, wherein your fathers have dwelt: and they shall dwell therein, even they, and their children, and their children's children for ever . . ."* This description of permanent residency did not occur. There was a substantial diaspora of the nation of Judah in 70 A.D. when the Romans obliterated

Jerusalem and most of its people. Those whom the Romans missed were eliminated in the Muslim invasion in the seventh century. Without a doubt, Ezekiel 37:25 has not been fulfilled.

Yet a third problem for Baron is found in Ezekiel 37:26, where it states, *"... and I will place them, and multiply them, and will set my sanctuary in the midst of them for evermore."* The sanctuary built in the days of Ezra and Nehemiah lasted only until A.D. 70. Since its complete destruction by the Romans, there has been no national sanctuary in Jerusalem to this very day.

It is obvious to any impartial observer that the return of the exiles in the days of Ezra and Nehemiah was not the great regathering spoken of by the Prophets. That event is still unfulfilled prophecy. The vast bulk of true, genetic Israelites remains scattered in the many nations of their dispersion, awaiting the return of Jesus Christ and the Spirit of God to stimulate that long anticipated action.

Objection #5: Modern Jews

Objection Stated: It is a commonly accepted historical fact that the people called Jews today are the only legitimate descendants of ancient Israel. Their return to Palestine in 1948 represents the prophetic regathering of Israel. Thus, any Caucasians claiming to be Israelites must be mistaken.

Answer: There are two branches of Jewry: the Ashkenazi and the Sephardic Jew. The Sephardic Jew traces his ancestry back through Spain and before that to Palestine. There is evidence that the Sephardic Jew may indeed be Israelitish in his genetics. However, the Ashkanazi are by far the larger part. In excess of 90% of the world's Jews are Ashkenazi, and they have no genetic link whatsoever to the Israelites of old. Since the vast bulk of modern Jews are Ashkenazi, it is not unfair to focus our attention upon them. We can thus state that nearly all modern Jews are not true Israel, but make that claim through either ignorance or fraud.

This is not a new circumstance. Indeed, the Revelation letter informs us that there have been and will be imitators claiming to be Jews: *" . . . I know the blasphemy of them which say they are Jews, and are not, but are the synagogue of Satan" (Revelation 2:9)*. Again, one chapter later, we read, *"Behold, I will make them of the synagogue of Satan, which say they are Jews, and are not, but do lie; behold, I will make them to come and worship before thy feet, and to know that I have loved thee" (Revelation 3:9)*. Not once, but twice, we are informed that there exist people who falsely claim to be Jews, that is, of Israelitish descent. Is it possible that the modern Jews of today could be these imitators? Absolutely. Please read carefully the following quotations made by respected scholars, all of whom are Jewish, except the last two. They will tell you that they are not Israelites.

"Strictly speaking, it is incorrect to call an ancient Israelite a 'Jew' or to call a contemporary Jew an 'Israelite' or a 'Hebrew'" (*Jewish Almanac*, p. 1, 1980).

"Political Zionism is almost exclusively a movement by the Jews of Europe. But these Eastern European Jews have neither a racial nor a historic connection with Palestine. Their ancestors were not inhabitants of the 'Promised Land.' They are the direct descendants of the Khazar Kingdom which existed until the 12th century" (Dr. Benjamin H. Freedman, *National Economic Council Inc., Council Letter #177*, October 15, 1947).

"Many [Jews] *of whom have clamored to go back* [to Palestine] *never had antecedents in that part of the world . . . The overwhelming majority of Jews are descendants from the converts of Khazaria and elsewhere who adopted Judaism . . .This view of the non-ethnicity of the largest portion of Jewry is sustained by such prominent anthropologists as Ripley, Weissenberg, Hertz, Boas, Pittard, Fishberg, Mead, and others"* (Dr. Alfred M. Lilienthal, "Middle East Terror—The Double Standard Address," *30th Anniversary Fund, Phi Beta Kappa*, 1985, p. 5).

"Genetically they [Jews] are more closely related to the Hun, Uigar, and Magyar tribes than to the seed of Abraham, Isaac, and Jacob. Should this turn out to be the case, then the term 'anti-Semitism' would become void of meaning" (Authur Koestler, *The Thirteenth Tribe*, New York, Random House, 1976, p. 17).

"The American people have been led to believe that Jews are 'God's Chosen People.' This myth was started by a small group of Jews . . . Leading the cry 'We are God's Chosen People' are the Zionist/Marxist Jews who for political purposes chose Judaism and who don't have a drop of biblical Jewish blood in them" (Jack Berstein, as told by Len Martin in *The Life of an American Jew in Racist Marxist Israel*, Costa Mesa, CA, Noontide Press, 1984, p. 6).

"The main part of Jewry never was in Judea, and had never come out of Judea" (H. G. Wells, *The Outline of History*, New York, MacMillan Publishing, 1923, p. 494).

And finally, a quote from Henry Ford Sr., perhaps the greatest industrialist in world history. Despite the fact that the media in recent decades has tried endlessly to malign his character, much of what he stated on this topic remains without successful rebuttal. *"The Jews are not the chosen people, though practically the entire church has succumbed to the propaganda which declares them to be so"* (*The International Jew*, 1921, chap. 2).

So it is clear that despite the popular assumption that modern Jews are the direct genetic descendants of ancient Israelites, careful research reveals that this is simply not true. Now, if modern Jewry is not of Israelite origin, where are the descendants of the Israelites today? Unprejudiced study of the Bible and history prove that the Caucasian race of Western Europe is true Israel.

Are You Courageous or Fainthearted?

I have attempted to prove to those who are open-minded enough to consider the facts of Scripture and history that the great bulk of the genetic descendants of ancient Israel are comprised today of the Caucasians in Europe, the United States, etc. Previous chapters have argued this point, I hope, persuasively. It has now been demonstrated here that this topic is relevant for the following reasons: first, modern Jewry is not really of Israelitish origin. Second, the regathering prophesied of old has not occurred, neither in Ezra's time nor in 1948. Third, the promises of the New Covenant have not been transferred to other people by grafting them in or adopting them to make them "spiritual Israel." Fourth, Jesus never sent His disciples in the Great Commission to evangelize every person everywhere, but rather sent them to *"go to the lost sheep of the house of Israel"* (Matthew 24:15), who were dispersed into all nations of the world. Finally, trying to sidestep this issue by ridiculously objecting to the facts of history is intellectually shallow and unworthy of serious consideration.

The simple fact is this: those of Caucasian European descent are Israel. This matters in both the spiritual realm and our tangible world. Are you courageous enough to act upon this information in any meaningful way, or will you brush it off like the fainthearted and politically correct?

11

Who Are Jews?
A Flowchart Study Tracing
the Descendants of Judah

*"We are all omnibuses in which our
ancestors ride, and every now and then one of them
sticks his head out and embarasses us."*
–Oliver Wendell Holmes

Today the word *Jew* can mean many different things, and depending on whom you are talking to, can stimulate a wide range of reactions. The confusion associated with this word is not new. Historians and the modern media have used it in different contexts and to refer to several groups of people. Even the Bible uses the word *Jew* in different contexts.

Historic and textual context is required to correctly understand the word. And, there is plenty of history behind the word. If one uses the nominal definition of *Jew*, meaning someone who is descended from the tribe of Judah, there have been 3,700 years of opportunity to make the term confusing!

To punctuate the thought that the Bible uses the word with both a positive and negative connotation, consider Revelation 3:9: ***"Behold, I will make them of the synagogue of Satan, which*** *say they are Jews, and are not, but do lie; behold, I will make them to come and worship before thy feet, and to know that I have loved thee."* From this passage (see also Revelation 2:9), we glean these vital thoughts: there were both *true Jews* and *false Jews* present when the Holy Spirit inspired John to write those words. Furthermore, since this was written in the future tense and plainly indicates that there will be a day when the true will be sorted from the false, and since that moment certainly has not occurred, the only conclusion that can be drawn is that there are still *true* and *false Jews* roaming around planet earth today.

The question that remains is this: can we identify the true *Jews*? Who are the legitimate descendants of Judah that hold the covenant blessings reserved for Judah? Conversely, who are the imposters? How did they manage to usurp the names *Judah* and *Jew* and a measure of the credibility that does not rightly belong to them?

The chart at the end of this chapter is an attempt to simplify the somewhat complicated 3,700-year history that has resulted in the confusion over the word *Jew*. Three thousand-plus-years is a long time. Much has occurred. The reader is cautioned to study the chart with that thought in mind. To be quite candid, this chart is actually a simplification of the historic reality, a thought that a casual observer might find surprising. Yet, it is also an honest attempt to trace all of the salient branches of the topic with enough completeness to satisfy most readers.

The King James Bible is the beginning point of this study. It is taken as a point of faith that the King James Bible needs no correction. The outstanding scholarship of the translators has never been equaled. That said, however, the translators understood their task was to translate, not interpret every shade of symbolic meaning. Their use of the word-for-word method of translation rather than the modern notion of dynamic equivalency resulted in honest and impeccable scholarship that guarded against the injection of subjective, interpretive thoughts. The use of concordances and lexicons is welcomed to amplify and further illuminate the meaning of a given word in the King James Bible, but not to replace or remove that word. Do not flee from the word *Jew*. Study the word and trust that the providence of God guided the translators.

Historic context is absolutely vital on a topic of this nature. When a word such as *Jew* is used, consider what was happening at the time of the event—say 500 B.C. Who was using the word, and what was its context? We must never assign a modern meaning to a word describing an event long ago. The connotations of words change in subtle and sometimes even dramatic ways. For example, the word *Indian* once only meant a person from India, and that is still the primary meaning to the British. But to an American, the primary meaning of the word *Indian* means the pre-Columbian inhabitants of North America, a very different group of people. Similarly, the term *American soldier* once referred almost surely

Both are called "Indian," but are quite different in race and culture. Similar ambiguities have plagued the word "Jew" through its 3,000+ year history.

to Caucasians only, but now the term carries no racial connotation at all; such a person could be White, Black, Hispanic, or even Asian. It speaks only to his geographical home. The word *Jew* has been subject to these same kinds of transitions. Specificity is required to avoid confusion!

Most of the dates assigned on the chart prior to A.D. 70 are taken from Ussher's *The Annals of the World*. Although some chronologists find fault with his work, it still remains one of the most complete histories of ancient times and utilizes more primary sources than most researchers today have readily available. Dates assigned subsequent to A.D. 70 are taken from disparate sources. The validity of the chart does not really hinge on the dates, but on the movement and activity of the people under study. In some cases, pinpointing the exact date of a broad movement of people misleads the reader into thinking that something happened overnight when in reality it took many years. The year is given as an estimate and a convenience for the reader.

As shown in the key, solid lines represent those descendants of Judah that have maintained a pure genetic profile. Dashed lines represent those who have either mixed their genetics through race mixing or are complete imposters and bear the name *Jew* without having any connection whatsoever to the man Judah, the son of Jacob. Multiple lines flowing to a box represent a large number of people numbering several million, perhaps even more. A single line represents a smaller quantity. However, sometimes a very modest population leaves a powerful imprint on the course of history. A case in point is the exiles taken to Babylon in 588 B.C. Jeremiah 52:30 reveals that the total number of persons taken was only 4,600. Yet they were the cream of the social order that were still alive after the war and constituted all the potential intellectual and mercantile leadership. Their absence in the land of Judah left only the broken, rural poor who had no real hope of maintaining a functioning commonwealth. It was only with the return of the exiles (now more numerous because of natural increase) that Judean nationhood was restored.

The most useful tool in sorting out the word *Jew* is to remember that it was originally a contraction of the word *Judah* and came into usage in the sixth century BC, only about a century before the last book of the Old Testament was composed. It is, therefore, no surprise that is appears only sporadically in the Old Testament narrative and only in the books that deal with the history of Judah just before the captivity and immediately subsequent to the same event. It is patently false to assume that those who are of pure, genetic stock are never called *Jews* and that the word *Jew* refers only to mixed race Judeans or those who are complete imposters. A case in point is Daniel 3:12 where Shadrach, Meshach, and Abednego are called *Jews*, but cannot possibly be genetically corrupted since they were previously identified as being members of the Davidic royal aristocracy in Daniel 1:3-7.

Thus, without any cut and paste formula that automatically tells us whether a given *Jew* is genetically authentic, we are forced to do the heavy lifting of research and study on a case by case basis. Context is everything when dealing with the word *Jew*.

By the time we reach the New Testament period, the words *Jew, Judah, and Judean* are used interchangeably by various writers and only tell the reader about the geographic origin of a given individual. No real assumptions can be made about his ethnic origins. As the centuries pass, writers and historians have used the word *Jew* more frequently, often with a negative connotation because it was the *Jews* who were responsible for the Crucifixion of Jesus Christ. But what kind of *Jews* were the ones most to blame for His death? Was it the true, pure descendants of Judah, men like Nicodemus and Jesus Himself? Or, was it mixed-race Edomites who were converts to the Hebrew religion but had a proclivity toward the perversion of the same? Or, were there elements of both that bear guilt? It may be hard to answer with perfect clarity, but knowing that both genetically pure *Jews* and genetically corrupted *Jews* were present on the scene is useful.

From the second to about the twelfth centuries AD, there is relatively little information about *Jews,* particularly compared to earlier periods. Historians have generally assumed that the Diaspora of *Jews* after AD 70 (which included both true and false *Jews*) resulted in their migration to two areas of Europe: Spain and Poland. It is in these two locations that they resurfaced after centuries of mysterious movement. There are distinct and important differences between them, but they both carry the baggage of the Talmud by this time (although different versions). Many people assume these two groups are the same genetically. That assumption is incorrect. Although there are a paucity of good sources that can fill in those blank centuries with the detail that would be desired, there is enough information to confidently assert that the *Jews* who emerged in Spain, known as Sephardic, are not the same as those that emerged in Poland and Eastern Europe, known as Ashkenazi.

The Sephardic are, for the most part, genetically true *Jews*, although certainly not Christian. The Sephardic *Jews* of Spain did not even know other *Jews* existed until the tenth century. Those others were the Ashkenazi *Jews*, descendants of the mixed race Khazars who were converted to Talmudic Judaism in the late eighth century by *Jews* from Babylon and Constantinople who were fleeing persecution. The racial amalgam of genetically false *Jews* from Babylon and Constantinople with the Khazars resulted in a large *Jewish* population in what is now Poland and the Ukraine by the thirteenth and fourteenth centuries. It is from this branch of false *Jews* that the Zionist movement sprang in the nineteenth century. It is also from the Ashkenazi, far more numerous than the Sephardic, that the vast bulk of modern Jewry comes—those who are now found in the United States and the Israeli state founded in 1948.

But it is not the tiny surviving branch of the Sephardic true *Jews* that represent the largest quantity of true descendants of Judah. The vast bulk of those who can legitimately claim the mantle of Judah, along with the covenant blessings thereof, are the Germanic-speaking people of central Europe. It was in the campaign by the Assyrians immediately following the fall of Samaria in 721 B.C., when the northern kingdom of Israel was taken into captivity, that many people of the southern Kingdom of Judah were also taken. Although the kingdom of Judah survived that near calamity, it was stripped of many inhabitants from the rural regions unable to retreat behind the walls of Jerusalem. Along with the northern ten tribes, many people of the tribes of Judah, Benjamin, and Levi were exiled. This large mass of Israelites eventually escaped the clutches of the cruel Assyrians by slipping across the Caucasus Mountains, after which they slowly made their way northwestward into Europe. Being stripped of their cultural background, they adopted heathen habits and became known in history as Goths, Saxons, Teutons, Vandals, and the other related Germanic tribes. By the third century before Christ, they had settled into their new home, the dark, forested lands of central and northwest Europe. The perilous crossing of the high passes of the Caucasus Mountains gave this race its name, the Caucasians. Among this race are found, by far, the largest bulk of true descendants of Judah. It is those who are the genetic offspring of the Germanic people of Europe that can therefore be correctly called *Jews*.

In everyday conversation, calling the Germanic descendants of Judah "*Jews*" will certainly confuse many people. As a practical matter, the word *Jew* today usually refers to the descendants of the Ashkenazi, a group of people with virtually no true genetic claim to the man Judah or his father Jacob. But facts are facts, and no matter how hard some will try to bury the truth, it has an uncanny habit of eventually resurfacing for the benefit of those who are patient.

For those who wish to study this topic for themselves, some of the best sources beyond Scripture are *Jewish Antiquities* by Josephus, *Annals of the World* by James Ussher, and *The Thirteenth Tribe* by Arthur Koestler.

The following pages display a flowchart that is useful in explaining the history of the terms, *Judah, Jew,* and *Judean*. Limited space forces the chart to be reproduced in a small format. To obtain a larger chart, write to *Watchman Outreach Ministries* at 3161 South 2275 Road, Schell City, MO 64783.

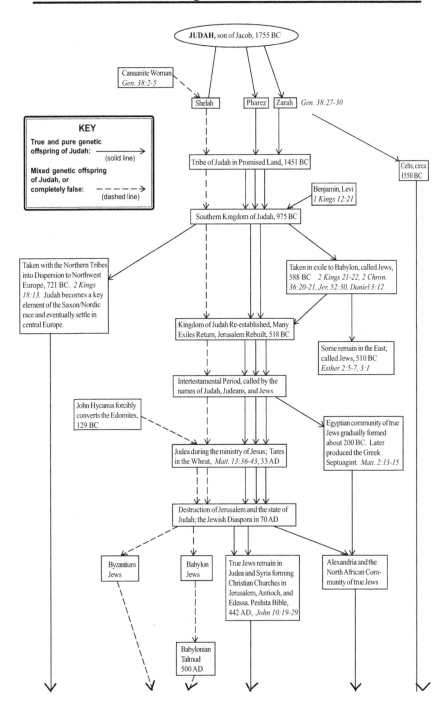

JUDAH, son of Jacob, 1755 BC

Canaanite Woman
Gen. 38:2-5

Shelah | Pharez | Zarah | Gen. 38:27-30

KEY

True and pure genetic
offspring of Judah: ————→
(solid line)

Mixed genetic offspring
of Judah, or
completely false: — — — — →
(dashed line)

Tribe of Judah in Promised Land, 1451 BC

Celts, circa
1550 BC

Benjamin, Levi
1 Kings 12:21

Southern Kingdom of Judah, 975 BC

Taken with the Northern Tribes
into Dispersion to Northwest
Europe, 721 BC. 2 Kings
18:13. Judah becomes a key
element of the Saxon/Nordic
race and eventually settle in
central Europe.

Taken in exile to Babylon, called Jews,
588 BC   2 Kings 21-22, 2 Chron.
36:20-21, Jer. 52:30, Daniel 3:12

Kingdom of Judah Re-established, Many
Exiles Return, Jerusalem Rebuilt, 518 BC

Some remain in the East;
called Jews, 510 BC
Esther 2:5-7, 3:1

Intertestamental Period, called by the
names of Judah, Judeans, and Jews

John Hycanus forcibly
converts the Edomites,
129 BC

Egyptian community of true
Jews gradually formed
about 200 BC. Later
produced the Greek
Septuagint. Matt. 2:13-15

Judea during the ministry of Jesus; Tares
in the Wheat, Matt. 13:36-43, 33 AD

Destruction of Jerusalem and the state of
Judah; the Jewish Diaspora in 70 AD

Byzantium
Jews

Babylon
Jews

True Jews remain in
Judea and Syria forming
Christian Churches in
Jerusalem, Antioch, and
Edessa. Peshita Bible,
442 AD, John 10:19-29

Alexandria and the
North African Com-
munity of true Jews

Babylonian
Talmud
500 AD

Continued from previous page . . .

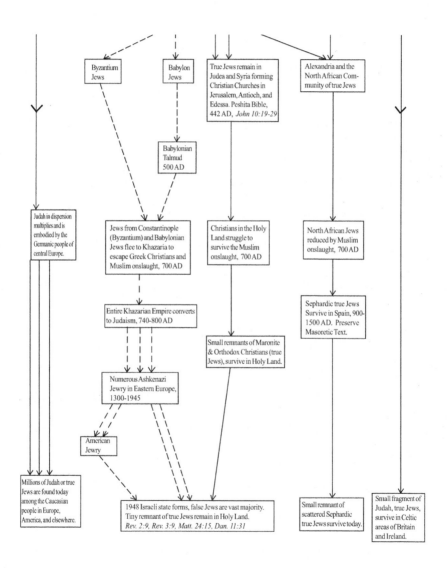

Byzantium Jews

Babylon Jews

True Jews remain in Judea and Syria forming Christian Churches in Jerusalem, Antioch, and Edessa. Peshita Bible, 442 AD, *John 10:19-29*

Alexandria and the North African Community of true Jews

Babylonian Talmud 500 AD

Judah in dispersion multiplies and is embodied by the Germanic people of central Europe.

Jews from Constantinople (Byzantium) and Babylonian Jews flee to Khazaria to escape Greek Christians and Muslim onslaught, 700 AD

Christians in the Holy Land struggle to survive the Muslim onslaught, 700 AD

North African Jews reduced by Muslim onslaught, 700 AD

Entire Khazarian Empire converts to Judaism, 740-800 AD

Sephardic true Jews Survive in Spain, 900-1500 AD. Preserve Masoretic Text.

Small remnants of Maronite & Orthodox Christians (true Jews), survive in Holy Land.

Numerous Ashkenazi Jewry in Eastern Europe, 1300-1945

American Jewry

Millions of Judah or true Jews are found today among the Caucasian people in Europe, America, and elsewhere.

1948 Israeli state forms, false Jews are vast majority. Tiny remnant of true Jews remain in Holy Land. *Rev. 2:9, Rev. 3:9, Matt. 24:15, Dan. 11:31*

Small remnant of scattered Sephardic true Jews survive today.

Small fragment of Judah, true Jews, survive in Celtic areas of Britain and Ireland.

12

True Jews and New Jews: Sorting the Authentic from the Imitators in World History

"It may well be that many East European Jews are descended from the Khazars; I may be one of them. Who knows?"
–Isaac Asimov

The previous chapter outlined some of the problems associated with the usage of the word *Jew* and offered some visual assistance in understanding how this confusion developed. A fuller discussion of this tangled history is now offered. Both of these chapters are explanatory in nature; it is suggested that the reader keeps the flowchart close at hand for reference.

Those who wish to understand what is going on in the Middle East, particularly the ongoing Israeli-Palestinian uproar, need a good dose of world history. Unfortunately, mainstream media sources are unlikely to provide any of the needed background to this seemingly never-ending, never-changing-much, never-quite-conclusive conflict. The truth can be ferreted out, however, for those who are willing to at least consider ideas that run against the grain of politically correct dogmas. But bear in mind, there is a good reason that most media networks consistently present only one perspective. There are powerful forces committed to suppressing the truth, hoping to bury it in an unmarked grave where generations to come will never find it. To unravel every aspect of this topic is beyond the scope of this book. Thus, this discussion will focus on only one singular thread in this large garment.

Biblical Who's Who

In one of the most remarkable stories in world history, there is a group of people who have assumed the identity of another. Loosely known as "Jews," these folks are not, in terms of strictest definition of the term, Jews at all. Most people assume that the terms *Jewish, Hebrew*, and *Israelite* are synonymous. They are not!

Briefly, let us consider these terms. A *Hebrew* is one descended from Eber, the great-grandson of Shem, Noah's son. More loosely it is sometimes applied to all the descendants of Shem (Genesis 10:21). However, the term Hebrew has been most often historically connected to the twelve tribes of Old Testament biblical Israel. An *Israelite* is certainly quite precise in its meaning and has not been used in looser contexts. It simply means the descendants of the man Israel, better known as Jacob. The twelve tribes, coming from his twelve sons, comprised the children of Israel. The term *Jew*, actually a latecomer to the Old Testament, originally and technically means one who can genuinely claim genetic descent from Judah, one of the twelve sons of Jacob. It is from the Hebrew word *Yehudi*, meaning *of Judah*. Please feel free to check your concordances and dictionaries to verify these facts.

These Judahites were a numerous and energetic tribe that eventually became a very dominant segment of the twelve-tribed Israelite Commonwealth. After the reign of King Solomon, the other tribes revolted from the tyrannical rule of King Reheboam, who was of the tribe of Judah. Reheboam and the tribe of Judah were left bereft of nearly all of their former countrymen. Primarily due to geographical reasons, the larger portion of the tribe of Benjamin could not join this revolt and thus remained under the dominance of Judah. Many Levites and a smattering of folks from other tribes were also retained. This truncated nation eventually was called the *Kingdom of Judah*, and the region it occupied *Judea*. All of its inhabitants, of whatever tribe, were often called Judeans, and in time *Jews*. However, never was the term *Jew* or *Judean* ever applied to the Northern Kingdom that had rebelled against Reheboam. The Northern Confederation was called the *Kingdom of Israel*,

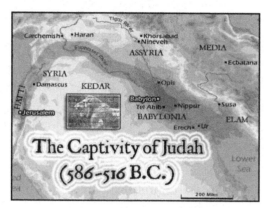

The Captivity of Judah (586-516 B.C.)

and its inhabitants were still called *Israelites*. As time passed, the Northern Kingdom was taken into captivity and scattered to the north and west (circa 721 B.C.). The Kingdom of Judah was later hauled off to Babylon (circa 586 B.C.), where many stayed. Seventy years later a remnant returned, and gradually, with much struggle, regained its status of nationhood. Unfortunately, the religion they returned with had picked up many pagan elements while in Babylon, and this gradually evolved into a system of oral interpretations that Scripture condemns as the tradition of elders (Matthew 15:2-3 and elsewhere).

Some New Jews

At this juncture in history, an unusual development occurred that muddled the meaning of the words *Judah*, *Judean*, and *Jew*. In the second century before Christ, a dynamic priest-king of Judah (John Hyrcanus of the Hasmonean dynasty) conquered the people directly to the south of Judah, the Edomites. The Edomites, later called Idumeans, were descended from Esau, Jacob-Israel's twin brother (Genesis 36:8). Esau had married a woman of a Hittite family, thus destroying forever the pure genetic pedigree of his descendants. For this Esau had been essentially disinherited (his mother saw the need for this before his father—see Genesis

26:34-27:46). These folks had been perennial enemies of both Israel and Judah since ancient times. Of them, the Bible has absolutely nothing positive to say (see Obadiah). After thoroughly subjugating them, Hyrcanus apparently thought he could get rid of them once and for all by giving them the choice of either death or conversion to the religion, language, and culture of Judah. This proved

John Hyrcanus, King of Judah, circa 150 B.C.

to be a catastrophic decision for the people of Judah, and a choice which Hyrcanus should have known was forbidden in Old Testament law (Deuteronomy 7:1-5, Leviticus 20:24, Joshua 23:12-13, Ezra 9:1-4, Nehemiah 13:23-30). Not surprisingly, most chose conversion.

The Jewish (truly of Judah) historian Josephus described this event: *"Hyrcanus took also Dora and Marissa, cities of Idumea, and subdued all the Idumeans; and permitted them to stay in that country, if they would circumcise their genitals, and make use of the laws of the Jews; and they were so desirous of living in the land of their forefathers, that they submitted to the use of circumcision, and of the rest of the Jewish ways of living; at which time this therefore befell them, that they were hereafter no other than Jews" (Jewish Antiquities, Book 13, 9:1).* The marginal note in Josephus' works adds this commentary, quoting Ammonius, a writer from A.D. 129: *". . . the Idumeans were not Jews from the beginning . . . but being afterward subdued by the Jews, and compelled to be circumcised, and to unite into one nation, and be subject to the same laws, they were called Jews."* Another editorial comment regarding Josephus' work adds emphasis: *"This account of the Idumeans admitting circumcision, and the entire Jewish law, from this time, or the days of Hyrcanus, is confirmed by their entire history afterward."*

The significance of the Edomite population merging with the Judeans is often overlooked. But it is not really any secret. Many modern biblical scholars admit that the historic event did indeed occur. For example: *"But during the warlike rule of the Macabees [Hasmonean dynasty of Judah] they were again completely subdued and even forced to conform to Jewish laws and rites and submit to the government of Jewish prefects. The Edomites were then incorporated into the Jewish nation, and the whole province was*

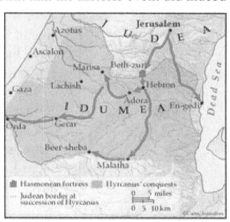

Hyrcanus' conquest of the Edomites or Idumea.

often termed by Greek and Roman writers 'Idumea' . . . From this time, the Edomites as a separate people, disappear from the pages of history" (The New Unger's Bible Dictionary, p.333). Even the encyclopedia on your shelf may inform you of these events, if one is sharp enough to understand the significance: *"The Hasmonean dynasty conquered the Idumeans in the 100's B.C., and converted them to Judaism"* (World Book Encyclopedia, 1967, vol. 6, p. 55)

Over the next century, as imperial Rome cast its long shadow over the Middle East, these Edomites, Or Idumeans, were gradually absorbed into Judean society. Many of them achieved high status, working their way into the priestly and aristocratic classes. Those that leveraged their way into the priestly professions had a strong proclivity for the pagan oral interpretations brought back from Babylon. Dominance in the two mainstream religious parties, the Pharisees and Sadducees, was soon theirs.

But the most successful among the Edomites was Herod. Through political marriages and devious machinations, he managed

to get the Roman imperial government to appoint him as the vassal king of Judah. Like many others, he was a Judean by geography, a citizen of the nation of Judah, a Jew in terms of language and religion, but was still an ethnic Edomite. His genetic background, the one aspect of his person that was utterly unchangeable, was not of Judah, nor even of Israel, and thus, in terms of race, could not possibly be defined as a true Jew! Herod is illustrative of the fact of this racial mixing and the tension it produced in Judean society, as revealed in this statement: *"The father of Herod the Great was a man of Idumean blood named Antipater . . . the Jews regarded the Idumeans with considerable suspicion and prejudice, calling them 'half Jews'"* (The New Unger's Bible Dictionary, p. 555).

Bust of Herod the Great from the first century B.C.

This was the situation when Jesus Christ lived and walked the lovely hill country of Galilee and Judea. There were two groups of people living cheek by jowl with each other in the land of Judea. They spoke the same language, practiced in their own fashion the same religion, suffered under the same oppressive yoke of Roman rule, and were together called Jews. But one group had a true ethnic claim to the terms *Judah* and *Jew*, while the others did not.

In A.D. 70, the city of Jerusalem and the Kingdom of Judah were utterly shattered. The Romans killed vast thousands, multitudes were sold into slavery, and still more were scattered throughout the Roman world, finding refuge where they could. A modest portion of this dispersed number were true followers of Jesus Christ who were absorbed into the Christian Church of the first several centuries. These were the wheat, alluded to by Jesus Christ in His parable of the wheat and the tares (Matthew 13). Before they blended into the church, these true Jews (of Judah) were known as Quartodecimans, which literally means "fourteenthers" because they wanted Passover to be celebrated on the fourteenth of Abib rather than on Easter Sunday. Meanwhile, the tares, comprised primarily of the Edomite element of these Jews, had utterly rejected Jesus Christ. They lodged themselves in various enclaves in the Roman Empire including Egypt, Spain, and Byzantium (later renamed Constantinople). During the centuries that followed, these people continued to develop and propagate their highly altered form of the ancient Hebrew faith in which the biblical aspects were almost completely submerged in layers of pagan philosophy and rules. It was during this era that their oral tradition was codified into a written textual form. Called the Mishnah, this was in turn commented upon and eventually placed in written form known as the Gemara. Together the Mishnah and Gemara comprise the Talmud, which has been the touchstone of the Jewish religion of Judaism for many centuries.

More New Jews

Judaism quite possibly would have expired in the tumult of the early Medieval Period had it not been for a single titanic evangelistic coup. In approximately A.D. 740, an entire empire was forcibly converted to Judaism by the decree of its emperor.

This was the Khazarian Empire, centered in modern day Ukraine, comprised of a people of mixed Turkish descent. The Khazarians took to their new faith like ducks to water. Even after their empire

dissolved, never to rise again, they retained tenaciously the precepts of Judaism. In the ebb and flow of nations and empires of that flat and open region, these proselytes to Judaism gradually made their way into Eastern Europe, where they settled in cities and took up commercial occupations. By the time the Medieval Period closes, they no longer considered themselves Khazarians, but they viewed themselves as Jews, for it was the religion of Judaism that formed the backbone of their subculture.

Bust of a Khazar warrior. Note the Mongol features.

Arthur Koestler, a prize winning Jewish author, summarizes these developments in his best selling book, *The Thirteenth Tribe*: *"Thus the Judaization of the Khazars was a gradual process which, triggered off by political expediency, slowly penetrated into the deeper strata of their minds and eventually produced the Messianism of their period of decline. Their religious commitment survived the collapse of their state, and persisted, as we shall see, in the Khazar-Jewish settlements of Russia and Poland"* (p. 74).

Other sources document this important historical event: *"The Jews, expelled from Constantinople, sought a home amongst them [Khazars], developed the Khazar trade, and contended with Mohammedans and Christians for the theological allegiance of the pagan people. The dynasty accepted Judaism (c. 740) . . ."* (Encyclopedia Britannica, 1911, vol. 15-16, p.775).

It is no mystery to the modern world that, as of a century ago, most Jews in the world were found in Eastern Europe, with the highest percentage concentration in Poland. How did they get there? A clearer picture is gradually emerging than what was heretofore available. Koestler continues: *". . . the cumulative evidence makes one inclined to agree with the consensus of Polish historians that 'in earlier times the main bulk originated from the Khazar country'; and that, accordingly, the Khazar contribution to the genetic make-up of the Jews must be substantial, and in all likelihood, dominant"* (p. 180).

It is from these proselytes to Judaism that the language of Yiddish developed. Yiddish is not Hebrew! While it does have some Hebrew words, which these Khazarian Jews picked up from the writings of the Pentateuch (first five books of the Bible), Yiddish has strong elements of Germanic, Slavic, Aramaic, Romance, and even Turkic languages. The polyglot background of this tongue is reflective of the multi-ethnic background of the Khazarian Jews as they migrated from the Eurasian steppes to eastern

The Khazar Empire at its peak in A.D. 850.

Europe. The noted Jewish writer A. N. Poliak believed Yiddish had its origin in Khazaria when he stated: *"The shape of early Yiddish emerged in the Gothic regions of Khazar Crimea"* (*Khazaria: The History of a Jewish Kingdom in Europe, p. 131*).

But what is most important to remember about these Khazarian converts to Judaism is this: they have no genetic link to Abraham,

Isaac, Jacob-Israel, Judah, or any other Hebrew. Furthermore, the great majority of all Jews today are descended from this Khazarian branch. While the small number of Edomite/Idumean Jews can accurately claim Abraham as their father through disinherited Esau, the Khazarian branch has virtually no genetic link whatsoever.

New Ambitions

A movement known as Zionism began in the late nineteenth century that still has significant impact on our world today. It was the notion that the Jews needed a homeland and nation of their own, preferably Palestine. The movement quickly became popular, despite the fact that nearly all Jews in the world had no genetic claim to Jacob-Israel or Judah. Indeed, only a modest number had ancestors who had ever dwelled in Palestine, and these were through disinherited Esau! Speaking pragmatically, the Hawaiians and the Haitians had just as valid a claim to Palestine as did these "Hebrews."

Undeterred, however, in 1917 the Zionist movement was able to convince the British Crown, in the midst of the stresses of

World War I, that they would be an asset to the British in the Middle East should the British prevail in the war. The British hoped to capture Palestine as a prize from the almost defeated Ottoman Empire, who had been the rulers of that region. This agreement, known as the Balfour Declaration, gave the Zionist movement the international respectability they

Theodor Herzl, founder of the Zionist movement.

needed. When the war ended, the British followed through and began to make space for the Jewish immigrants by relocating the Palestinian Arabs. The process slowly continued for the next three decades.

After World War II, Jewish militants began a violent campaign targeting British and Palestinian leaders and strongholds. They wanted their own government—complete independence. In 1948, the erstwhile terrorists became statesmen, and the modern nation of Israel came into existence.

On July 22, 1946, the Zionist terrorist organization *Irgun* bombed the King David Hotel in Jerusalem, British government headquarters, killing 91. *Irgun* was the forerunner of the *Likud* party, which has dominated Israeli politics since 1977.

Of course, the 1948 regime calling itself Israel has a flimsy claim to that word! While most people presume they are genetic descendants of Abraham, in truth, most are not; and those that are, can only claim so through Esau, who was, one must not forget, disinherited! Actually, none of them are descendants of Jacob-Israel, whose name they have pilfered. Furthermore, none of them are from the tribe of Judah, and thus have no right to the term "Jew," at least in its original sense. Do these people then have a legitimate genetic claim to the land they presently occupy? Clearly not.

Do they have a religious claim? Modern Judaism is primarily built upon Talmudic principles and gives only remote lip service to the Penteteuch. Additionally, they have zero connection to the life, ministry, and teachings of Jesus Christ, whom they openly repudiate. And interestingly, many modern Jews are ironically quite secular. While they keep one foot connected to the culture adopted by their "Jewish" forebears, many are openly atheistic or at least agnostic. Any religious claim to Palestine is nil.

The vast majority of those that reside today in the modern nation of Israel are impostors. Twice in the book of Revelation the followers of Christ are informed that there exists a group of people who claim to be Jews, but are not: *" . . . and I know the blasphemy of them which say they are Jews, and are not, but are the synagogue of Satan"* (Revelation 2:9, see also Revelation3:9). For those who wish to be honest with the totality of Scripture, there is no mistake—somewhere on this emerald blue planet of ours, there is a group of people who claim to be Jews, but are actually not.

So, can we find these people who claim to be Jews, but are actually quite adversarial to Jesus Christ as Savior and Lord? For anyone bold enough for unfettered thinking, the conclusion is painfully obvious. Those occupying Palestine today, the Israelis, fit this biblical description perfectly. Despite the lavish but naïve enthusiasm of American evangelicals for these people, most of them want nothing to do with Jesus Christ! Nearly all of them repudiate His name, His teachings, His reputation, and only tolerate His followers as long as they can profit from doing so. Of all people, these that are today called Jews have a well-earned reputation for indifference and often hostility to the name of Jesus Christ.   Therein lies the incriminating, identifying evidence.

True Israelites

Scripture provides many indicators that will shed more light upon the matter. On these we will touch briefly, although much could be written. Those who are true Jews (genetic descent of Judah) or are true Israelites (genetic descent from Jacob-Israel) will have certain distinguishing marks that have characterized them through the centuries. Early on, the Bible tells us for what to watch. *First*, they will be a numerous people (Genesis 22:17). Those folks in Palestine claiming to be Israel have always been small in number. By contrast, the true Israelites, the Anglo-Saxon people have always been highly fruitful and numerous. *Second*, true Israel will be a nation and a company of nations (Genesis 35:11). While this accurately fits the Anglo-Saxon peoples, the impostors have not constituted a nation through almost all of their history, not to mention a company of nations. *Third*, a crown, that is royal ruling house, will always be found among true Israel (Genesis 49:10). Indeed, the current British monarch, Elizabeth II, can trace her ancestry directly to the house of David in Scripture, which is a fascinating topic already addressed in this book. The charlatans in Palestine do not have a royal house at all, let alone one that can prove its biblical pedigree. *Fourth*, there will always be a lawgiver (priestly or ministerial order) found in true Israel (Genesis 49:10). Such a direct link can be found in the history of the church in the Britain, again a riveting historical study. The false Jews in Palestine cannot produce a reasonable connection. *Fifth*, true Israel will be known by a new name (Isaiah 62:2, 65:15). Prophetic fulfillment in this area is obvious. These few marks, however, are but a beginning of the scriptural clues that reveal who are the wheat and who are the tares!

Perhaps one of the most compelling studies that proves that Anglo-Saxon Christians are true genetic Israel is found in Revelation 12. A quick survey of this chapter will be fruitful. Begin by observing verses 1-2: *"And there appeared a great wonder in heaven; a woman, clothed with the sun, and the moon under her feet, and upon her head a crown of twelve stars: And she being with child cried, travailing in birth and pain to be delivered."* It is clear that this woman must be ethnic Israel, the twelve crowns being the key indicator. The child whom she was delivering under great historic duress was Jesus Christ. Continue in Revelation 12 by looking at verses 5-6: *"And she brought forth a man child, who was to rule all nations with a rod of iron: and her child was caught up unto God, and to his throne. And the woman fled into the wilderness, where she had a place prepared of God . . .*" The man child destined to rule all nations is plainly Jesus Christ, Who did indeed ascend into heaven. Meanwhile, this woman, Israel, fled into the wilderness. What does this mean? It is a description of true ethnic Israel as they found safety in the wilderness portions of the earth—northwest Europe and later North America—wilderness regions at that time. Now resume in Revelation 12 by looking at verse 17: *"And the dragon was wroth with the woman, and went to make war with the remnant of her seed, which keep the commandments of God, and have the testimony of Jesus Christ."* The dragon is Satan. With whom is he angry? The woman, who is Israel. And what are the hallmarks of her remaining descendants? They keep God's commandments and adhere to the gospel of Jesus Christ. Now, in all honesty, does this description fit the people today commonly referred to as the Jews? No! More often than not, they are actively supporting the ACLU and others who despise the commandments of God. And, of course, most of them openly repudiate Jesus Christ as the divine Son of God. On the other hand, this is a very fine description of historic WASPs—White Anglo-Saxon Protestants. Even today, what people are found leading the battle for the Ten Commandments and esteem the name of Jesus Christ? Is it not still Anglo-Saxons? The Caucasian people are those who have the marks of true genetic Israel.

Understanding Current Events

In order to understand the events of the Middle East today, you must know who Israel is! And, also important, who Israel is not! Those commonly known as Jews today are not Israelites! They have no ethnic claim to the land of Palestine. They have no religious claim to the land of Palestine. The Palestinian people have a better claim than they, for the Arabs have been squatting on the land for many hundreds of years. But, the true claim, the real Israelites, the people with whom God made an everlasting covenant, are the Caucasian Christians of Europe and America.

When the British surrendered their lawful and biblically legitimate claim to the land in 1948, the usurpers stepped forward. Now the world is witnessing a strange phenomenon: the two contenders battling it out over Jerusalem and Palestine, the Arabs and the Jews (so called), are both squatters! No clarity will emerge in the Middle East as long as the identity confusion reigns. We look forward to the day when Jesus Christ will return, separate the wheat from the tares, remove the imitators, and restore the inheritance of the Holy Land to its rightful heirs.

A Note from the Author

*"Even if you're on the right track,
you'll get run over if you just sit there."*
–Will Rogers

M y intent in this book is to present a lucid, easy-to-read compilation of the essential elements of the Anglo-Israel thesis. It is evident that the implications of this truth are many, both on a personal level and for Western Civilization. Many who read this book will readily admit that our society is moving in a direction that is frightening. Even as I write, Barack Obama has just been elected to a second term, a shock for many considering the poor record of his first four years in office. Among White Americans there is a new sense that we have been largely disenfranchised. Our first Black President only curried favor with very select groups among Caucasians simply because the demographic changes in our nation have made a broad appeal unnecessary. It is becoming evident that we have reached the proverbial "tipping point," and the United States of America may never return to its cultural foundations.

Some believe that this is merely a cultural issue and has nothing to do with ethnicity. They are mistaken. With the demise of White America, biblical Christianity will also be swept from the field of battle. Oh yes, Christianity per se will survive, but it will not be rooted in Scripture, nor will it retain the substance and flavor of historic Christian theology. Other races will continue to adapt elements of Christian practice to suit their needs, but it will not be the same. It is only with true, genetic Israel that God has established His unique covenant relationship. With the rarest of exceptions, it is only among Caucasians you will find the bearers of biblical Christianity, the culture we now see slipping from our grasp. It is the loss of racial identity that has resulted in this crisis.

Do not construe my comments as desiring evil, harm, or hardship toward any race or ethnic group. I seek only to rekindle a sense of honor and purpose for my own ethnic kindred through the dissemination of truth.

For Caucasians in the western world, the foreseeable future looks grim. Yet, Israelites have faced conditions that have been worse, and God has opened windows of opportunity. Remember how our ancient ancestors were utterly crushed by the Assyrians, taken as captives to a foreign land, only to escape and begin anew! This book has presented an object lesson of God's enduring faithfulness to His Israelite people and should provide a glimmer of hope for those who feel discouraged.

What you do with this information is, of course, up to you. But if you do nothing at all, my effort has been in vain, and this knowledge will be of absolutely no value to you. It has been my experience that when presented with the ideas offered here, some acknowledge its validity, but find that the cares of daily life slowly tarnish its lustrous gleam until it is obscured from vision and nearly forgotten. This must be resisted if you are to retain the marvelous bequest from your Israelite forefathers!

There are a number of excellent books published in the last century that expound in greater detail many of these themes.

For those with the time and inclination to study further, you are encouraged to do so. The bibliography contains only a very modest sampling out of the several thousand works that could be potentially accessed. For additional copies of this book you can order online at Amazon.com, write to *Watchman Outreach Ministries* at 3161 South 2275 Road, Schell City, Missouri, 64783, or call (417) 432-3119. May God's blessing be upon your life.

Reed Benson
January 2013

Bibliography
and
Recommended Works

Abbadie, Jaques, *Le Triomphe de la Providence et de la Religion.* London: 1723.

Allen, John Hardin, *Judah's Sceptre and Joseph's Birthright*, London: Paradise, 1902.

Anglo-Saxon Chronicle. New York: Fordham University Press, 1994.

Angus, Joseph, *The Bible Handbook.* Grand Rapids, Michigan: Eerdman's Publishing Company, 1982.

Apocrypha. New York: Oxford University Press, 1977.

Belloc, Hilaire, *The Battleground: Syria and Palestine.* London: J. B. Lippincott Company, 1936.

Bennett, W. H., *Symbols of Our Celto-Saxon Heritage.* Windsor, Ontario: Herald Press Limited, 1976.

Blodgett, Terry, *Similarities in Germanic and Hebrew.* Salt Lake City: University of Utah Press, 1982.

Bright, John, *A History of Israel.* Philadelphia: Westminster Press, 1981.

Camden, William, *Britannia.* London: 1557. Facsimile Reproduction, Elibron Classics, 2004.

Capt, Raymond E., *Missing Links Discovered*. Muskogee, Oklahoma: Artisan Publishers, 2011, 1985.

——————, *The Traditions of Glastonbury*, Thousand Oaks, California: Artisan Publishers, 1983.

Chronicles of the Kings of Britain. Reprinted London: McCarthy Company, 1892.

Collins, Steven, *The Lost Ten Tribes of Israel Found*. Boring, Oregon: CPA Books, 1992.

Dalin, Olaf von, *Svearikes Historia, Volume 1*. Stockholm: 1747.

The Declaration of Arbroath. New York: Penguin Books, 1993.

Dickey, C.R., *One Man's Destiny*. Merrimac, Massachusetts: Destiny Publishers, 1951.

Encyclopedia Brittanica, 11th Edition. New York: Encyclopedia Brittanica Incorporated, 1911.

Eurenius, Johannes Jacobi, *Atlantica Orientalis*. Strengnas: 1751.

Fell, Barry, *America B.C.* Muskogee, Oklahoma: Artisan Publishers, 2005.

Finkelstein, Louis, *The Jews: Their History*. New York: Judaica Press, 1977.

Ford, Henry, *The International Jew*. Originally published in "The Dearborn Independent," 1921.

Freedman, Benjamin H., *National Economic Council Documents*. New York: 1947.

Gay, Peter, and Wexler, Victor, *Historians at Work.* San Francisco, Harper and Row Publishers, 1975.

Gayman, Dan, *The Covenants of the Bible.* Schell City, Missouri: Watchman Outreach Ministries, 1998.

——————, *The Theocratic Kingdom.* Schell City, Missouri: Watchman Outreach Ministries, 2011.

Gildas, *De Excidio et Conquestu Britanniae (The Ruin and Conquest of Britain).* Sixth century A.D. Oxford: Reprinted, English Historical Society, 1838.

Goard, William Pascoe, *The Post-Captivity Names of Israel.* London: Covenant Publishing, 1934.

Govett, R., *English Derived from Hebrew.* London: S.W. Partridge and Company, 1869.

Gray, Andrew, *The Origin and Early History of Christianity in Britain.* London: Skeffington and Son, 1897.

Haberman, Frederick, *Tracing Our Ancestors.* Muskogee, Oklahoma: Artisan Publishers, reprint of original,1934.

Hawtin, George, *The Abrahamic Covenant.* Thousand Oaks, California: Artisan Publishers, 1988.

Hjelmslev, Louis, *Language, an Introduction.* Copenhagen: Blue Waters Press, 1960.

Jewish Almanac. New York: Alfred A. Knopf, 1980.

Jewish Encyclopedia. London: Harper Collins, 1960.

Johnson, Edward, *Johnson's Wonderworking Providences of Sion's Savior in New England.* London: 1630.

Johnson, Warren, *Abraham, Father of Many Nations.* Santa Clarita, California: Christosoro Publishing, 2001.

Josephus, Flavius, *Jewish Antiquities.* Grand Rapids, Michigan: Kregel Publications, 1999.

Jowett, George, *The Drama of the Lost Disciples.* London: Covenant Publishing, 1980.

Koestler, Arthur, *The Thirteenth Tribe.* New York: Random House, 1976.

Lilienthal, Alfred M., "Middle East Terror—the Double Standard Address," *30th Anniversary Fund, Phi Beta Kappa.* New York: Phi Beta Kappa, 1985.

Loyer, Pierre le, *The Ten Lost Tribes Found.* 1590.

Luckenbill. D.D., *The Ancient Records of Assyria and Babylon.* New York: Doubleday Press, 1961.

Martin, Len, *The Life of an American Jew in Racist, Marxist Israel.* Costa Mesa, California: Noontide Press, 1984.

Martin, Walter, *The Kingdom of the Cults.* Minneapolis: Bethany House Publishers, 1985.

Mather, Cotton, *The Ecclesiastical History of New England.* London: 1702.

Milton, John, *The History of Britain.* London: 1670.

Monmouth, Geoffrey, *History of the Kings of Britain.* London: Eggleston, 1909.

Morgan, Richard, *Saint Paul in Britain or The Origin of British Christianity.* London: 1860.

Morton, Nathaniel, *New England's Memorial.* London: 1669.

Mozeson, Isaac, *The Word: the Dictionary that Reveals the Hebrew Source of English.* New York: Shapolsky Publishers, 1989.

Poliak, A.N., *Khazaria: The History of a Jewish Kingdom in Europe.* Tel Aviv: Mossad Bialik, 1951.

Prichard, James, *Eastern Origin of Celtic Nations.* London: Delphi, 1857.

Rawlinson, Henry, *The Origin of the Nations.* London: Blackwell & Sons, 1921.

Shriek, Adrian van der, *Troost Mijn Volk.* Rotterdam: 1614.

Smith, Charles, *Palestine and the Arab-Israeli Conflict.* Boston: Bedford/St. Martin's Press, 2001.

Thompson, J.A., *The Bible and Archaeology.* Grand Rapids, Michigan: Eerdman's Publishing Company, 1962.

Turner, Sharon, *The History of the Anglo-Saxons.* Paris: Baudry's European Library, 1840; Elibron Classics Replica, 2003.

Unger, Merrill F., *The New Unger's Bible Dictionary.* Chicago: Moody Press, 1988.

Ussher, James, *The Annals of the World.* Green Forest, Arkansas: Master Books, 2003.

Wells, H.G., *The Outline of History.* New York: MacMillan Publishing, 1953.

Weiland, Ted, *God's Covenant People.* Scottsbluff, Nebraska: Mission to Israel Ministries, 1997.

Weisman, Charles, *Who Is Esau-Edom?*. Burnsville, Minnesota: Weisman Publications, 1996.

Wilson, J., *Our Israelitish Origin: Lectures on Ancient Israel*. Philadelphia: Daniels and Smith Company, 1850.

World Book Encyclopedia. Chicago: Field Enterprises Educational Corporation, 1967.

Worrell, William, *A Study of Races in the Near East*. University of Michigan Press, 1927.

Yadin, Yigael, *Biblical Archaeology Review*, "Mediterranean Hebrew Colonizers," Volume 41, Number 3.

Made in the USA
Las Vegas, NV
30 June 2022